WHY VOTE CONSERVATIVE 2015

WHY V●TE 2015 CONSERVATIVE

NICK HERBERT

Biteback Publishing

First published in Great Britain in 2014 by
Biteback Publishing Ltd
Westminster Tower
3 Albert Embankment
London SE1 7SP
Copyright © Nick Herbert 2014

ISBN 978-1-84954-736-9

10 9 8 7 6 5 4 3 2 1

A CIP catalogue record for this book is available from the British Library.

Set in Chaparral Pro

Printed and bound in Great Britain by
CPI Group (UK) Ltd, Croydon CR0 4YY

For Jason, a true Conservative

Contents

Foreword

This book is not an account of the Conservative Party's achievements in government, or a compendium of its policies. Others will produce that, and there is a strong story to tell. Conservatives can be proud of what has been achieved by a government that inherited from Labour the worst deficit in peacetime history: bringing spending under control and restoring economic growth; capping welfare; reforming schools.

Instead, the aim of this book is to reflect on the challenges facing this country, and suggest how the next Conservative government should apply its principles to deal with them.

A general election will soon be held. It is easy to see the dangers of Labour forming the next government, with the inevitable undoing of our achievement in rescuing the country's economic fortunes. We must not let that happen. And a major part of the agenda for the next Conservative government is clear: a referendum on Britain's membership of the EU within three years, and continuing action to deal with the deficit.

But what else? Conservatives yearn for majority government; to be able to kick the Liberal Democrats all the way down Whitehall. Now we must be clear about what we would do with this power.

It has been said that the Conservative Party exists to hold power, as though this could license an administration without purpose. It could not. Conservatism exists, as Quintin Hogg wrote, 'for the sake of promoting the good of the country'.[1] But so, he noted, do

---

The Case for Conservatism, 1947

other parties. We therefore have to explain the good we wish to do, why our vision is better, and why it is more likely to succeed than that of others.

It is also said that, after the defeat of socialism, we have entered a post-ideological age, in which voters care little for the claims of capitalism against collective provision, but simply wish to see the country run well. Yet there are enduring ideological differences fundamental to the choice facing the public. The left's blind faith in the state allowed school standards to fall unchecked; it promoted generations of welfarism that trapped the weakest in poverty; it caused the excessive public spending that brought this country to the edge of bankruptcy.

If a previous Labour leader, Tony Blair, attempted to persuade his party that collective provision could not endure, his current successor has no such mission. Ed Miliband is the most left-wing Labour leader since Michael Foot: hostile to markets in the private sector, even more so to those in public services; unrepentant in his support for higher spending, taxation and borrowing; unreconstructed in his support for the welfare state. He supports deeper European integration and opposes a referendum on the EU. There is indeed an ideological choice at the next election, and we must frame it clearly.

It will not be enough, however, to point to the dangers of a Labour government, real though they are. We must also set out our stall. That requires us to assess the problems facing the country, and say how we will fix them. Today, in an age of disillusionment with politics, the greatest danger lies in saying only what we think the public want to hear. People are not only deaf to promises without conviction, they deeply mistrust them. It is not just our responsibility to say what we believe, it is the only way to win a hearing.

Our case should be that Britain is facing serious challenges that conservatism is best placed to meet. Only if we continue to fix the economy and ensure global competitiveness will living standards be protected. This requires much more than standing still and managing public services well. With an ageing population, rising costs and ever higher public expectations, nothing less than a transformation of the welfare state and public services is needed.

In this book, I argue that conservatism does not apply a single ideology to contemporary problems. As John Buchan said, Conservatism is 'above all things a spirit not an abstract doctrine'.[2] We can identify principles that should guide us as we shape a modern Conservative agenda. But we must not repeat our opponents' mistakes and claim that a single doctrine can right every wrong.

To take just one example, we need more houses; it is clearly right to extend opportunity. But we must also protect the countryside. This reflects the tension which exists in so many policy choices because of the rival claims of Conservative principles.

If we ignore the failures of the planning system, we will fail a generation for whom property ownership is becoming an ever more distant dream. But if we lazily conclude that planning restrictions simply need tearing up, we will fail future generations by destroying the national asset of the countryside. The Conservative solution will acknowledge the force of both claims. It will turn an eye to people's needs now, and propose reforms, while being sensitive to the reasons that saw the introduction of planning controls in the first place.

The Conservative writer Graeme Archer eloquently expressed the importance of this tension in the Conservative condition, describing himself as 'a mixture of gloom for what has gone and optimism for the future ... Two horses pull the Tory chariot: the trick is not to allow either to pull us out of kilter.'[3]

The most powerful moments in the most recent chapter of our party's history have been when we have re told Conservative truths. When David Cameron spoke of aspiration; when George Osborne liberated pensions; when Iain Duncan Smith challenged welfarism

---

2   Preface to A. Bryant, *The Spirit of Conservatism* (1929), p. vii, quoted in *Ideologies of Conservatism*, E. H. H. Green, 2002

3   Article on ConservativeHome, 14 August 2014

or when Michael Gove drove through education reforms, our hearts beat faster, not because we knew that these policies were right, but because they spoke to our core beliefs. Holding to Conservative ideals, it turns out, energises our party and is popular in the country. As my colleague David Willetts, author of an earlier edition of *Why Vote Conservative* and a leading thinker about modern conservatism, has said, 'Mrs Thatcher's government showed that the Conservative enjoys the luxury of being able to stick to his principles knowing that they also work in practice.'[4]

It was a new incarnation of conservatism, more than three decades ago, which rescued this country from what some thought was terminal decline. Today's economic and political challenges are different, but equally profound. In the age of fierce globalisation, no country has an entitlement to success. But if we have the courage to take the right decisions now; if we are willing to apply our principles, a regeneration of conservatism can once again ensure Britain's prosperity.

Chapter 1

Introduction

Conservatism is a disposition not an ideology. It rejects the intellectuals' conceit that it is possible, let alone wise, to bring about radical change 'upon a theory'[5] in favour of a solid grounding in history and experience. The Conservative temperament demands that we should recognise that the world is too complex and too diverse to be ruled by a single principle, and that even, or perhaps especially, in times of tumultuous change, we have a duty to proceed with caution as we consider the radical changes that may be necessary for our society. The Conservative opposes revolution, not change. Benjamin Disraeli put this most clearly:

> In a progressive country change is constant; and the great question is not whether you should resist change which is inevitable, but whether that change should be carried out in deference to the manners, the customs, the laws and the traditions of a people, or whether it should be carried out in deference to abstract principles, and arbitrary and general doctrines.[6]

This may not appeal to the tidy minds of the men whom Edmund Burke decried as 'sophisters, economists, and calculators',[7] but it

---

5   Edmund Burke, *Reflections on the Revolution in France*, 1790
6   Speech in Edinburgh, 1867
7   Burke, op. cit.

focuses on something much more important: the quality of people's lives and government's role in making these better.

Ours is a globalising age. Ideas, technology, money and people move faster, farther and more cheaply than they ever have. Each of the main parties is defined by its reaction to it. UKIP fears the change as a threat. Labour denounces it as a platform for exploitation. Liberals welcome it as a blessing. We should embrace it as a fact. Globalisation brings huge benefits, while at the same time inflicting insecurity on people unequipped to deal with the increasing intensity of competition it brings. Our job in politics is to equip Britain and her people to meet its challenge.

This challenge cannot be met by a list of policies alone. It requires careful thought and honest reflection. Labour's years in office inured voters to spin, and they rightly seek substance. We must follow a style of politics that conveys our intent and philosophy. Promises that are unanchored by a set of beliefs will founder; they will leave us without a clear direction; and they will leave the public with no idea of our motivation. We need to supply voters with an account of the principles that will guide us.

These principles, or values, are the root of our thinking. The values that inform conservatism are timeless, though the combination in which they are found and the compromises we make between them, in a spirit that pays respect to our cardinal virtue of responsibility, are modern. Each of the six principles which this book identifies – Nation, Security, Liberty, Community, Equality and Opportunity – provides a reason to vote Conservative.

Britain is once again emerging from a major economic crisis. Globally, it is generally considered to be the most profound since the Great Depression, but the last serious British economic crisis, which occurred in the 1970s, was also under a Labour government. In the modern era, where voters call for Conservatives when the economy needs fixing, we must never forget the importance of fiscal responsibility. It is vital not because economic performance is always the most important issue facing the country, but because good economic performance is a prerequisite for providing people with opportunity, contributing to global security, reducing crime and preserving our quality of life. A successful economy generates the wealth that allows people the security to plan for the future; it makes the products and services we enjoy; and it allows society, through moderate taxation, to marshal resources to help those less fortunate, to preserve our heritage, to safeguard the environment and to foster scientific discovery. It is essential to a civilised society.

Securing good economic performance is less a matter of knowledge than of will. Preserving sound money, low taxes and a market economy, all under the rule of law, depends on responsibility, Conservatism's cardinal virtue. It requires politicians to resist the temptation to borrow when we cannot afford to pay back, impose high taxes when we cannot safely borrow, and undermine the market economy with regulation and political intimidation when we cannot tax. It is more important than ever to be able to exercise that discipline. The world economy is in the middle of another extraordinary transformation, a global revolution, that is dramatically changing how business is done, how customers are satisfied, how products are supplied and how services are rendered. A global 'premier league' is being formed, in which the rewards for participation far exceed those confined in national divisions. At issue is whether Britain can secure her place in it, whether her citizens can be protected from its threats as well as take advantage of its benefits, and whether the prosperity it generates can be shared fairly among them.

The next chapter of this book sets out the considerable challenges facing Britain. The following chapter examines modern Conservative values, and subsequent chapters explain how each of the values selected informs policy proposals to meet the challenges. The final chapter sets out the choice facing the country at the next election.

Chapter 2

The Challenge

We are living through a seismic transformation of the world economy and its societies: globalisation. Its roots are twofold: first, in technological change and, second, in its successful exploitation by newly independent countries, particularly in east Asia, who made good use of their independence. Those that have chosen to run themselves well have taken over the mass industrialisation pioneered in the West, brought their people prosperity beyond all precedent and dramatically lowered the cost of living for their Western customers. It has opened up huge opportunities for wealth, cultural enrichment and scientific progress as the peoples of the world are brought much closer together. But it has come at the cost of enormous dislocation in the leading Western economies and great insecurity for our most vulnerable citizens on which populists (in Britain, Labour as much as UKIP) thrive. Moreover, the sheer increase in global industrial output, in demand for food and water, and in the ease with which people can travel, has put immense strain on our climate and natural resources, as well as Western nations' social welfare systems and immigration policies.

Not all countries, however, have seized the opportunities that the modern world offers them. In far too many cases their new rulers proved venal, corrupt, or, seduced by the illusory spoils of war, roused their people into destructive nationalistic ideological or religious fervour. The blood-soaked consequences of misgovernment laid waste to Cambodia and Rwanda and are presently being felt in Iraq. Extreme political incompetence or corruption has always bred discontent and revolution, but globalisation makes the instability impossible to confine. Jihadists travel to Syria's wars. Images of massacre spur calls to international action. Distant upheavals up-end the fortunes of internationally ambitious companies, eliminating their investors' savings and putting people at home out of work.

These crises have provoked two contrasting and equally inadequate responses. Some believe that the causes are merely technical, most notably, poverty and ignorance. They promise salvation through technical means: the transfer of resources and knowledge and enlightened scientific research alone. Others claim that alien, sometimes violent, cultures cannot be reconciled with our own, and counsel a return to splendid isolation as the surest means of security. Yet it is clear from humanity's experience since the Second World War that political wisdom can overcome both ignorance and poverty: the advance of first South Korea and Taiwan and then China and India as they dismantled destructive economic systems has been astounding, and it is still only decades since the most civilised countries in the West descended into barbarism never exceeded elsewhere. Nor is it viable to pull up the drawbridge: not only would we thereby deny ourselves the opportunities that this fast-globalising world provides us – opportunities that will certainly accrue to others if we do not take them – but also we cannot by isolation secure ourselves against the threats it poses.

This chapter will identify eight major challenges for the United Kingdom which globalisation either brings or exacerbates:

First, a demographic time-bomb created by a pay-as-you-go welfare state in which we are ageing without saving.

Second, increasing regional inequality as London takes a full part in globalisation while other regions are left behind.

Third, excessive levels of public spending and debt that have created a high tax burden.

Fourth, fierce global competition that requires government to reduce taxes, deregulate, provide better infrastructure and improve skills.

Fifth, a technological revolution that will require the state to re-shape the way it provides services.

Sixth, high levels of immigration and population growth that have caused public disquiet and placed pressure on public services.

Seventh, environmental changes and pressure on natural resources that will affect our prosperity.

Eighth, and finally, world disorder which threatens our national security.

1. Ageing without saving

The acute banking crisis may be over, yet the most serious financial problem facing Britain is its long-term fiscal sustainability. Our population has been ageing without saving. The projections are striking:

> Better health is creating an increase in life expectancy in many countries around the world. Together with falling birth rates, this is contributing to an ageing population. The UK is no exception. According to the Office for National Statistics, the number of people aged sixty-five and over in the UK has already increased by 26 per cent since the mid-1980s – to 10.8 million in 2012. The number of people aged eighty-five and over more than doubled over the same period to 1.4 million and the percentage aged under sixteen fell ... Population ageing is projected to continue for the next few decades ... By 2037 the number of people aged eighty-five and over is projected to be 2.5 times larger than in 2012 ... The population aged sixty-five and over will account for 24 per cent of the total population in 2037, while the proportion of the population aged between sixteen and sixty-four is due to fall.[8]

---

8   'A tax system fit for the future: An economic perspective on Tax Reform', PwC, 2014

Both public and private debt have already reached astonishing levels. Public sector net debt is currently £1.3 trillion (77.3 per cent of GDP)[9] and household debt is at 165 per cent of GDP.[10] Around two-thirds of household debt consists of mortgages,[11] whose outstanding value is concentrated in London and the south east, where house prices are extremely high compared to earnings. This increases both the amount of debt (and indebtedness relative to incomes) needed to own a home, and the risk that, should house prices return to their long-run average levels, people would suffer from negative equity. Both as a nation and as individuals, we continue to live beyond our means. Where private debt is an obligation that people choose to undertake, public debt is different. It entails a promise by the government to bondholders that it will impose the taxes on future generations who did not benefit from the public services used, and who in many cases were not old enough to vote for the government that authorised the expenditure. It is a major intergenerational injustice.

The political system has compounded these risks by enacting promises in the form of fiscal transfers to the old through the state pension and the ring-fencing of budgets for public services that are mostly used by them, most notably the NHS. This predicament will only become more acute as the population ages and pensioners live longer, while at the same time the advance of medical technology has a double effect: not only is it increasingly expensive as more sophisticated and expensive treatments are made available and then come to be expected, but also its success contributes to extending life expectancy. The issue is not the fact of this progress, but the difficult question of how the money to ensure it is to be found, and how a sustainable fiscal framework that does not impose unbearable costs on future generations is to be developed.

---

9   ONS, Public Sector Finances June 2014, 22 July 2014
10   Bank of England, Financial Stability Report, June 2014
11   Ibid.

This generation of pensioners may point out that they have paid into the system, and this claim cannot be dismissed. Even though national insurance pay-outs are no longer related to payments received as pensions,[12] in an approximate sense the claim is true: they have paid their taxes during their years of work. But they only paid enough to support the previous generation of pensioners at the time at which they were working, as well as the other public functions discharged by the state at the time. Their taxpaying behaviour was consistent with an assumption that their children would be able to pay for them in their retirement, as they themselves had for their parents, without saving for their own living and healthcare costs in old age. The UK chose not to finance pensions through a contributory mechanism, or healthcare through a form of social insurance. It encouraged a mindset where people were reassured that the state would take care of their needs. But this pay-as-you-go system of social security is no longer viable.

Policy changes have made calculations of trends in state pension spending complex, but the expansion in the proportion of the nation's wealth devoted to healthcare has been significant. As a share of government spending, the NHS budget has increased by 42 per cent in the last twenty years.[13] If this rate continues, it will account for over a third of all government spending by 2054. In addition, the state pension currently accounts for £104 billion each year. This compares to £37 billion for incapacity benefit (which is disproportionately used by working-class men between the ages of forty-five and sixty-four),[14] £26 billion on housing benefits and £5 billion on unemployment benefit. The government's welfare reforms have already made significant progress towards improving the incentives to work and reducing the benefit traps that encourage dependency.

---

12   As explained in *Tax By Design*, Institute for Fiscal Studies, 2011

13   In 1993/94 the NHS accounted for 12.7 per cent of total managed expenditure. It now accounts for 18 per cent. (Public Expenditure Statistical Analyses, HM Treasury, 2014)

14   Individual budgetary figures from PESA 2014. Data on the demographic breakdown of incapacity benefit recipients from *Tax by Design*

The introduction of the Universal Credit will improve the situation further. Further short-term fiscal savings from benefit reform will be required, but the principal aim of the policy is to enable people to take control of their lives, escape dependency, earn money through work and develop self-respect. This will yield results over the long term as people remain in work and take advantage of the opportunities this offers them. The major costs of social protection are, and will continue to be, those associated with state pension provision.

State provision of pensions and healthcare free at the point of use, both financed through pay-as-you-go taxation, have nevertheless established strong expectations in the British people. It would be wrong to dash those expectations and impose the shock of financial hardship on people who would find it exceptionally difficult to cope, as their earning years are behind them. But if steps are not taken soon to reform the basis on which social protection is ensured in future, the chronic fiscal crisis will become acute. During a future recession, a government whose borrowing will have by then become too great could be forced to impose sharp tax rises and spending cuts in order to maintain the confidence of the bond markets. Reform is necessary to forestall the risk of future hardship.

2. Regional inequality

We are, in too many respects, not one nation. Britain's regional inequalities are stark. Annual Gross Value Added[15] per head in London, the richest region, is £37,232, whereas in the Tees Valley it stands at £14,710. As the difference between regions in the sources of household income show, the state attempts significant redistribution of income to even these inequalities out. The difference in the sources of household income bears this out. Whereas in London only 10 per cent of household income comes from benefits, in the north

---

15   GDP can only be measured nationally. Gross Value Added, however, can be measured on a regional basis.

east and Wales the figure is almost double, at 19 per cent.[16] Further redistribution is carried out by providing public services accessed for free. In the north east, a further 12 per cent of income is classified as being in the form of a 'free' public service or benefit, whereas in London only 7 per cent of income is.[17] Meanwhile, residents of the north east derive only 9 per cent of their income from profit, while Londoners derive almost twice as much.[18]

This inequality is often attributed to the failure or underperformance of, for instance, the north of England. One think tank notoriously suggested the region should be abandoned.[19] This is profoundly wrong. London's success should inspire us to work out how other regions of the country can join it in sharing the fruits of globalisation. London, a city in decline after the post-war period, has grown into the largest and richest in Europe by some distance, and this is reflected in its entrepreneurial spirit. What has it done right, and how might England's other great cities replicate it?

Though it now prospers thanks to globalisation, London was initially hit extremely hard by the same economic forces that have laid other regions low. Excessive union power and the invention of containerised shipping rendered its huge docks, once the British Empire's gateway to the world, obsolete. At the same time, the east Asian tiger economies, some of them former British colonies, began to compete in earnest with the Western manufacturing industry. Unfortunately for Britain this transformation of the global economy occurred when our own economy was in the middle of its disastrous post-war experiment in socialism that, before 1979, Conservative governments were unable, or unwilling, to unravel. Nationalised industries found it impossible to adapt. Powerful trade unions prevented the introduction of modern labour practices, and when they did not get their way,

---

16   The figures in this paragraph all derive from ONS, Income and Source of Income by UK Countries and Regions, 2010/12.

17   ONS Income and Source of Income by UK Countries and Regions, 2010/12

18   Ibid.

19   Oliver Hartwich et al., 'Cities Unlimited', Policy Exchange, 2008

brought the country to a halt with strikes and power cuts. Rather than adapting to this new world – taking advantage of technological changes to develop new industries and sectors, exploiting Britain's location, levels of education and the English language, and capital-ising on the country's famed spirit of enterprise (derided though it had been by Napoleon) – British governments tried instead to prop up loss-making nationalised industries, sufficient subsidies for which could not be extracted from an increasingly narrow tax base, even when confiscatory tax rates of 83 per cent (98 per cent on 'unearned' income) were imposed.

National economic collapse was avoided thanks to the successful reforms that Margaret Thatcher enacted, but the shock to established industrial centres, when it came, was severe. It was felt particularly strongly during the 1983 recession, and later when coal mines were closed. The measures taken were drastic, but there was no alterna-tive to what former Communist countries, attempting to correct misallocation of resources on a similar scale, described as economic 'shock therapy'. Britain in many ways faced the same problems of politically distorting, inefficient industry that crippled the econo-mies of the Soviet bloc and posed tremendous challenges for German governments after their country's reunification in 1990.

But even two decades later, not enough has been done to deal with the effects of Britain's failed mid-twentieth-century socialist experi-ment. New centres of economic activity have arisen, most notably in London's financial sector, but also in high technology on the M4 corridor and near Cambridge. Seizing the opportunities available in today's globalising economy, new industries have brought immense prosperity to the United Kingdom. But there is still considerable poverty, even amid the affluence, both in London's inner city and more widely in the south east.

And outside of London and the south east the renaissance has been much smaller in scale. Pockets of excellence exist, for instance in Derby's high technology manufacturing sector, Sunderland's revived car industry, Manchester's media production hub or the Sanger life sciences centre in Newcastle. The centres of England's northern cities have experienced an extraordinary revival, defying expectations of terminal decline. Yet the once great engines of capitalism that pioneered the industrial revolution remain overly dependent on the public sector. Even in Manchester, where the revival has been most conspicuous, just 10 per cent of income can be attributed to the profits of enterprise, compared with London's 17 per cent.[20] Moreover, despite possessing numerous excellent universities, these cities are unable, especially outside areas of the public sector such as healthcare, to generate significant numbers of the high-paying private sector jobs that sustain an advanced economy.

3. Spending without reform

If the problems of Britain's unsuccessful regions were due to twentieth-century socialism, New Labour squandered the opportunity provided by the long boom of 1994–2008 with policies that resembled the '21st-century socialism' championed by contemporary Latin American populists. During Labour's time in office, public expenditure grew sharply. By 2009, annual government spending had increased by £277 billion above the level necessary to keep pace with inflation[21] – more than twice the £133 billion spent to bail out failing banks.[22] Throughout its time in office, Labour cumulatively spent £1.5 trillion more than if government spending had only increased in line with inflation.[23] Had these revenues been economic rents

---

20 ONS Income and Source of Income by UK Countries and Regions, 2010/12

21 Public Expenditure Statistical Analyses, HM Treasury, 2014

22 National Audit Options, 'Taxpayer Support for UK Banks: FAQs', accessed August 2014. The UK also agreed to stand behind the banks in the event of further collapse, but did in fact have to make use of those guarantees

23 Figures calculated from *Public Expenditure Statisical Analyses*, HM Treasury. 2014, Total Managed Expenditure long run series (Table 4.3). Figures are for 'current' spending only and exclude expenditure on infrastructure, except some acquired expensively through PFI

from some renewable but concentrated resource, the policy might be justified on grounds of social justice. Instead, temporary revenues from a highly cyclical source of revenue were used to affect a permanent expansion of public spending. When those revenues collapsed, so did the government's income, and fiscal retrenchment became unavoidable.

Over the years Labour were in power, government spending grew from 39.9 per cent of GDP, which they inherited from the Conservatives in 1997, to 47.9 per cent in 2009/10.[24] This was the fastest spending growth of all OECD countries bar South Korea. Whereas in 1997 the UK had the twenty-second largest public spending share of GDP in the OECD, by 2009 it had the eighth. It had gone from spending less than Portugal, Italy, Greece and Spain, to spending more than each of them. According to OECD figures, Labour spent at a rate of 3.5 percentage points *higher* than the Greek government.[25]

Labour's level of spending endangered the fiscal stability of the country, while imposing an additional annual tax burden of £1,400 per household.[26] The money was not well spent: the productivity of government spending, as measured by the ONS's Centre for the Measurement of Government Activity, fell by 15.5 per cent.[27]

Some saw the dangers. In 2002, Reform warned:

> Without radical change, the government's colossal increases in public spending are programmed to fail. The economy as a whole will suffer; the credibility of public services will be damaged irreversibly; Britain's competitiveness in world markets will suffer significantly and real incomes will be reduced ultimately at every level of society.[28]

---

24 Robert Chote, Rowena Crawford, Carl Emmerson and Gemma Tetlow, '2010 Election Briefing Note No. 5: Public Spending Under Labour', Institute for Fiscal Studies, 2010

25 Figures for 'General Government Outlays as percentage of GDP' as above

26 'Tax and Benefit Reforms Under Labour', Institute for Fiscal Studies, 7 April 2010

27 Chote et al., op. cit.

28 'Spending without Reform: Interim report of the Commission on the reform of public services', Reform, June 2002

But most voices in the Conservative Party were silent. A disastrous and defensive new mantra took hold: that Labour's unbridled spending could not be challenged. Only when the financial collapse occurred did the party rediscover its belief in wise spending.

This government took office with public spending that had been planned to reach 48.1 per cent of GDP, the highest level since 1982/83, and a budget deficit exceeding one tenth of GDP. It has taken resolute action to reduce it through necessary spending restraint and some limited tax rises. By 2015 the deficit will be considerably less than half the level at which it was inherited, as a proportion of GDP, and government debt is expected to peak in 2015/16 at 78.7 per cent of GDP.[29]

Labour's high taxes and high spending are a brake on ambition, growth and enterprise. Not only do high taxes dissuade people from working or starting businesses, they subordinate huge shares of activity to the less efficient state sector. As Professor Tim Congdon has argued: 'The state churns citizens' money pointlessly in the so-called "systems" of tax-collection and benefit-disbursal, and is a wasteful, low-quality supplier of services that should be left to the private sector.'[30]

In 1913, when the British Empire ran a quarter of the world, the British state spent 12.7 per cent of GDP. Of course, the modern welfare state was introduced after this, but even in 1960 public spending was just a third of GDP. This is only slightly less, as a proportion of national income, than the 36.3 per cent Australia spends now.[31] When the Conservative government left office in 1997, with Ken Clarke as Chancellor, spending was on a downward trend as a share of GDP and fell to below 35 per cent in 2000/01 before Labour's spending boom began.[32] Spending has massively outstripped tax receipts in

---

29   Economic and Fiscal Outlook, Office of Budget Responsibility, March 2014

30   'The Case for Halving the Size of the State' in 'Reform: The Next Ten Years', Reform, 2012

31   OECD Statistical Database, General Government Disbursements, 2014 Forecast

32   HM Treasury figures

every year since. Though the government is bringing it back under control, it will not fall below 40 per cent until 2017/18.

Continued restraint on public spending will be needed to restore the public finances and reduce the tax burden in future. Hard choices will be needed but these will not be enough. The modern state will require a radically reformed welfare system and public services to ensure that we meet demands and pay our way.

4. Global competition

Other countries have leaner states. The pace of international competition is intensifying, and we need to do everything we can to ensure that Britain is best placed to take part and gain the benefits from the latest round of globalisation. This requires a continuous effort to improve our competitiveness. There are four main areas where Britain's performance needs major improvement: first, our tax burden is too high; second, regulation continues to impede business; third, infrastructure is provided too slowly; and fourth, we need to improve our skills base.

The government has made significant progress in reducing the tax burden, despite having to deal with the deficit. It has increased the personal tax allowance to £10,000, frozen fuel duty, cut corporation tax to a highly competitive 20 per cent and introduced an employers' national insurance allowance of £2,000. Nevertheless, levels of taxation remain too high. As the Institute for Fiscal Studies has shown,[33] there are three income taxes in Britain (which the Chancellor has considered merging in a future Budget):[34] actual 'income tax' plus two types of national insurance. Though the latter is divided into contributions assigned to the 'employee' and 'employer', this makes no economic difference. What matters to business is how

---

33   *Tax By Design*, Institute for Fiscal Studies, 2011
34   'Britain's Osborne may merge income tax and national insurance', Reuters, 30 June
      2014

much they have to spend in order for a worker to receive a particular wage. When all three taxes are taken into account, as much as three-fifths of the cost of employing someone who pays the 40p rate of 'income tax' (4.9 million people now pay tax at this rate) may be owed to the state.[35] Taxes are so high because the public sector has grown so large. It is not only that the state will be unaffordable in the future as the population ages: the public sector is a huge burden now. It needs to be reformed so that the tax burden can come down.

Second, excessive regulation wastes extremely large amounts of money. The Institute of Directors (IoD) has estimated that the administrative burden of regulation costs business £112 billion each year, or 7.9 per cent of GDP,[36] more than the entire education budget. This figure excludes the deadweight loss from profitable activities not undertaken because the regulatory burden is too large. Furthermore, a culture of gold-plating persists. As the IoD reports, even in the Business, Innovation and Skills department 'there is still considerable work to be done to change the culture of regulation in government, among civil servants, government lawyers who often adopt an extremely cautious approach in their advice, and also some ministers'.[37]

Conservative ministers have been determined to cut red tape. Adrian Beecroft developed imaginative and radical proposals to reduce employment regulation, through compensated no-fault dismissal, but these were opposed by the Liberal Democrats.[38] A 'one in, two out' rule now requires the abolition of two regulations before another is enacted, and a Deregulation Bill is before Parliament.

There is, however, no surer way of removing regulation than reducing the area in which government is active. Where this is not possible,

---

35   Steven Swinford, *Daily Telegraph*, 30 April 2014

36   'Regulation Reckoner', Institute of Directors, 2011

37   'The Midas Touch: Gold-Plating of EU Employment Directives in UK Law', Institute of Directors, 2013

38   Adrian Beecroft, 'Employment Law Review Report', Department for Business, Innovation and Skills, 2012

politicians should see their mission as improving Britain's business competitiveness, and reducing the regulatory burden, not increasing it. Despite rising to tenth place on the World Bank's Ease of Doing Business ranking,[39] the UK's performance is held back by key bottlenecks, most of which relate to local planning and interface with regulated utilities. The issue is not so much cost as speed. World Bank researchers had to wait fifty-six days for planning permission, an additional twenty-one days for their premises to be checked by a fire safety officer and a further twenty for it to be connected to water and sewage. Securing a connection to the national electricity grid was by far the slowest, taking 126 days, compared to sixty in the United States and eighteen in Korea. The German planning system was far quicker: the building permit was processed in twenty-five days and the fire inspection was carried out within twenty-four hours. It is not enough to accept our tenth place overall ranking. We need to learn from, and out-compete, the best-performing countries in the world.

Third, our infrastructure remains inadequate, and we provide it too slowly. In this highly competitive global economy we need the infrastructure to allow business to succeed, but short-termism and delays prevent it from being delivered. Labour proposed High Speed 2 (HS2), but has persistently flirted with cancelling it. The line will not reach Manchester and Leeds until 2046. Quite apart from the Channel Tunnel, cancelled by the Labour government in 1974, the British stretch of High Speed 1, connecting London to Paris, was delayed for years; the French completed their section a decade ahead of us. By contrast, Japan's regional cities thrive by being better connected. They invested in their 'Shinkansen' bullet trains in 1964. Now, while short-sighted opponents of HS2 in our country still call for its cancellation, Japan is planning new, even faster lines.

Crossrail, shortly to be completed, had been planned as early as 1979. An airport planned for the Maplin Sands in the Thames Estuary

---

39   World Bank Ease of Doing Business Ranking. Data obtained from www.doingbusiness.org

was cancelled in 1974, even though planning permission for it had already been obtained. We clearly need a major hub airport; now that the Airports Commission has ruled out the Thames Estuary, expansion at Heathrow is the only real option and must go ahead. Securing major infrastructure requires vision, political will, long-term prioritisation for capital spending (which, since thought unseen, is all too frequently the first victim of emergency spending reductions) and sufficient certainty to minimise investment costs.

Fourth, Britain's skills must improve. The government has put in place impressive education reforms, but there is still a lot more to do to enable our young people to compete in the rest of the world. The UK's performance in international standardised tests is exactly at the OECD average. British pupils fare significantly worse than those in Poland and Germany and are far behind those who score highest, in Shanghai and Singapore.[40] Both employers and university lecturers warn that too many children leave school unable to perform adequately at work or in higher education. We cannot afford to stand still while other countries advance. A Federation of Small Businesses survey found that nearly 30 per cent of small companies report skills shortages as a barrier to growth, and that the number is rising.[41]

5. The technological revolution

An information and communications technology revolution is transforming the way goods and services are provided across the globe, but it is leaving government and public services behind. As Reform has noted:

> The welfare state was designed more than half a century ago. Britain
> was a different country. Food was rationed. The average life expectancy

---

40   OECD, PISA test results, 2012
41   Federation of Small Businesses index, Q1, 2014

was about fifty (it is eighty today). Only one in eight married women worked. Heathrow Airport did not exist. The nation's economy depended on coal and steel.

Today's empowered consumers expect to make choices over all aspects of their lives. Progress over the last thirty years has been staggering. In 1972, less than half the population had a telephone and nearly two thirds didn't have central heating...

Yet in areas such as healthcare and education, choice for all but the richest 10 per cent of society is extremely limited. This is not an accident. Choice was designed out of a system based on collective funding and collective consumption.[42]

In a world of sophisticated consumers, where people expect information, choice and control at their fingertips, the centralised British state and monopolistic public services are poorly equipped to respond. New technology is transforming the delivery of services in the private sector, disrupting old, inflexible, centralised forms of business and replacing them with new, flexible, diverse and superior ways of working, communicating and entertaining. Only if services in the public sector are liberated from bureaucratic control will they be able to innovate and take advantage of these opportunities.

Technology could revolutionise criminal justice, allowing the sophisticated tracking of offenders. It could revolutionise healthcare, allowing the remote consultation and diagnosis of patients, or the monitoring of personal health and wellbeing. It could revolutionise transport, enabling the pricing of road use to replace road taxes. The list goes on. The opportunities to put people in control of processes that will improve the services they receive and reduce their costs are enormous. As John Micklethwait and Adrian Wooldridge have observed: 'Technology has even bigger potential ... than management. The internet has revolutionised everything that it has

---

touched, from the newspaper business to retail. It would be odd if it did not also revolutionise the state.'[43]

Yet the very structure of the modern state makes it deeply resistant to the changes needed. In the private sector the revolution is being driven by the market, by the forces of competition and the desire to make profits. The public sector, which under Labour grew to around half of the economy, is mostly immune from such pressures. Until now, the focus of reform has been on public services, with governments since Tony Blair's attempting – generally at the margin – to introduce choice and competition into public services. There is a great deal further to go. But there also needs to be a new focus on the machinery of government itself: on its ability to enable the reform needed; on the way it designs and commissions services; on how it measures value and controls costs. This is not just a matter of reducing its size: the centre needs to be re-shaped. As Micklethwait and Wooldridge also argue, 'The main political challenge of the next decade will be fixing government.'[44]

6. The shrinking world

Globalisation and technological change have made it much easier to travel. In 1971, a return flight from London to Sydney cost £7,154 and one to Nairobi £3,651 at today's prices.[45] Today, British Airways offers return flights to Sydney for around £1,700 and to Nairobi for approximately £550. In four decades, prices have fallen by more than 75 per cent in real terms. These huge reductions in cost have led to a corresponding increase in travel for tourism, trade and migration. Though few people object to increased tourism, increased migration has sparked major concern in all developed countries.

43   John Micklethwait and Adrian Wooldridge, *The Fourth Revolution: The Global Race to Reinvent the State*, 2014

44   Ibid.

45   Figures from M. H. Cooper and A. K. Maynard, 'The Price of Air Travel', Institute for Economic Affairs, 1971, adjusted by the GDP deflator

In part as a consequence of the operation of supply and demand, with the exception of Japan, all rich nations have developed multicultural societies. People have been attracted by the developed world's security, wealth and economic opportunity. Migrants have started one in seven of all existing businesses in Britain.[46] At the same time, the settled population (including, quite often, the last but one group of immigrant arrivals) have feared that new arrivals would take their jobs or welfare benefits, undermine the cohesion or nature of society, or put too great a strain on the social services and sheer capacity of the country to accommodate them.

Though being felt strongly here, these tensions are not peculiarly British. They have also been felt intensely at different times in France, Germany, Belgium, Spain and Italy, and they even recur frequently in the United States and Canada. Because they so easily involve matters of ethnic affiliation and religious identity, they can too easily be exploited to foment intolerance, division and hatred. Responsible political leaders have a duty to bring calm reason to this debate.

But they must also set the right policy framework. Net migration to the UK nearly quadrupled from 48,000 in 1997 to 185,000 in 2003. After eastern European countries were granted free movement in 2004, it peaked at 273,000 in 2007. Net foreign migration between 1997 and 2010 totalled nearly four million, two-thirds of it from outside the EU.[47] It is hardly surprising that an increase in migration and population on this scale should have caused concern.

There are a number of sources of public anxiety in the UK. Hatred or bigotry should of course be condemned in the strongest possible terms. Over the centuries Britain has been enriched by waves of immigrants, and the same is true of other major English-speaking nations. We have a long history of offering sanctuary to people fleeing persecution, from the Huguenots to the Ugandan Asians expelled by

---

46 'Migrant entrepreneurs: building our businesses, creating our jobs', Centre for Entre-
     preneurs at the Legatum Institute, 2014
47 Figures from Migration Watch UK

Idi Amin. We should celebrate that tradition and continue it in the future. Today, we should be playing our part in offering sanctuary to those fleeing from persecution in Syria. But there are respectable causes of concern that require a more complex response. People are worried about immigrants' effects on the labour market and the welfare system. Those who come to live in this country should do so because they admire it and want to make the most of the opportunities it offers, not cut themselves off from it, or worse still, plot to undermine our democracy. Finally, rapid influxes of people make it hard for communities to adjust and for public services to cope, while continuous sustained increases in population put pressure on our natural environment, architectural heritage and the fabric of our towns.

Concerns that an influx of labour (particularly cheaper labour) will displace a local labour force are economically similar to fears that new technology will displace workers. Large-scale studies of correlations between immigration and wages find little effects of significant magnitude in either direction.[48] Nevertheless, it does not make sense to import labour while paying for people to remain out of work. Welfare-to-work programmes are an important part of the answer to concerns about immigration.

People are also extremely concerned about the possibility of benefit tourism. Though the patterns of migration from the new European Union member states (generally young single people looking for work) are such that they make minimal demand on the welfare system (a recent European migrant is 50 per cent less likely than a member of the native population to make use of the benefit system),[49] this has not always been the case with immigration to Britain. A UCL study concluded that 'whereas EEA immigrants have made an overall positive fiscal contribution to the UK, the net fiscal balance of non-EEA

---

48   'Migrants in Low-Skilled Work', Migration Advisory Committee, 2014
49   Christian Dustmann and Tommaso Frattini, 'The Fiscal Effects of Immigration in the UK', Centre for Research and Analysis of Migration, UCL, 2013

immigrants is negative, as it is for natives'.[50] Moreover, it is conceivable that migrants may come here with the intention to work, but fail to secure it, and so end up drawing welfare benefits without having contributed to financing them. This is possible in the UK because of the unusually universal nature of the British welfare safety net, which through its pay-as-you-go financing also contributes to Britain's long-term fiscal problems. Moving to a contribution-based system would address both problems simultaneously.

A further serious challenge posed by increasing migration concerns capacity for this island to accommodate a higher population. There are two aspects: a question of flow, and of absolute numbers. A sudden increase, even of economically productive immigrants, will require adjustments to be made. They need houses, roads and hospitals, schools for their children, and other public services. They are likely to concentrate in particular areas which are not always easy to identify in advance, and some groups will find it easier than others to adapt to local cultural norms.

Not all of the projected population increase will be due to migration, but this is expected to account for a substantial proportion of it. According to Migration Watch:

> The UK population is projected to grow by over 9 million (9.4 million) in just twenty-five years' time, increasing from 64 million in 2013 to 73 million by 2039. Of this increase, about two thirds is projected to be due to future migrants and their children – the equivalent of the current populations of Birmingham, Leeds, Sheffield, Bradford, Manchester, Edinburgh, Liverpool, Bristol, Cardiff, Newcastle, Belfast and Aberdeen.

The Home Secretary, Theresa May, should be credited for substantial reductions in migration from outside the EU, which is now at its lowest levels since the 1990s. As a result, overall net migration has

---

50   Ibid.

fallen by a quarter since its 2005 peak, from 320,000 to 243,000.[51] But recent increases in net migration from EU countries such as Spain mean that the government is a long way from its target to reduce net migration to the tens of thousands. The problem with such a target is that the flow of migrants from within the EU into the UK is not within the control of the government, while net migration by definition also depends on the flow outwards.

Nevertheless, Migration Watch calculates that to keep the population of the UK below 70 million by the middle of this century, net migration must fall to around 40,000 a year. In the absence of such a reduction, the Office for National Statistics expects Britain's population to grow to around 77 million by 2050.

Population growth on this scale will further increase the demand for housing, disproportionately affecting regions like the south east where supply is already too low. The Home Secretary has said that more than a third of all new housing demand in Britain is caused by immigration.[52] The Mayor of London's Infrastructure Plan 2050 warns that 1.5 million new homes will need to be built in the capital alone by 2050, to accommodate a projected 37 per cent population increase to 11 million.

Migration has escalated to become one of the public's become biggest concerns, and it is imperative to address the issue.

7. The perfect storm

Globalisation's effects extend beyond the narrow economic sphere: they have had profound effects on the environment. The immense transformation in the economic fortunes of billions of people in the emerging world, as well as the advanced developed countries, has brought humanity unprecedented prosperity and unimaginable

---

51   Home Office news release on ONS figures, 28 August 2014
52   Theresa May, speech on 'An immigration that works in the national interest', 12 December 2012

improvements in people's standard of living. It has, however, inevitably been accompanied by vastly increased pressure on global environmental resources.

The most high-profile of these is greenhouse gas emissions, leading to climate change. The change is real, and the effects of failing to mitigate it or adapt to it would be dangerous for the UK and for the world as a whole. Climate modelling is a complex scientific endeavour, and it is necessarily difficult to predict the exact changes that an increase in the strength of the greenhouse effect will produce. As the effects derive from an increase in the amount of the sun's energy trapped by the atmosphere, they are not limited to an increase in average temperature, although they include that. Particularly serious consequences include the possible disruption of the monsoon season in south and south-east Asia, affecting the agriculture that feeds billions; the acidification of the oceans, rendering them uninhabitable for marine life; and the melting of the permafrost in Canada and Russia, expected to release methane (itself a greenhouse gas), thus causing a further intensification of the greenhouse effect. Furthermore, the seas will rise, slowly and inexorably, even years after carbon emissions are brought under control.

With the exception of sea-level rises, which will require improved flood defences, the short-term effects of climate change on the UK will be less disastrous. Britain, however, is only an island in the literal, geographical sense of the word. Quite apart from the humanitarian issues, our prosperity depends on trading with a prosperous and growing world, not one beset by major environmental calamity. With globalisation comes a vital interest in addressing global environmental problems. As Margaret Thatcher said, 'Stable prosperity can be achieved throughout the world provided the environment is nurtured and safeguarded. Protecting this balance of nature is therefore one of the great challenges of the late twentieth century.'[53]

---

53   Speech to the Royal Society, 22 September 1988

As with much environmentalism, many of the measures taken to attempt to deal with the problem have been inspired by the left, leading to two disastrous errors: the solutions themselves either do not work or are more costly than necessary. But too much of the right has taken refuge in denial of climate science. Rather than devote their energy to developing policies that go with the grain of human nature and harness the transformative power of capitalism, too many of the right's thinkers have preferred to sweep the problem under the carpet. This is, however, irresponsible and unconservative. We need to face up to the challenge that the expansion of industrialisation to what was once called the Third World has come to pose.

Climate change is only the most salient of our environmental challenges. As people in the emerging world continue to achieve higher standards of living, their demands on the planet's resources will increase. They will want more fresh water for drinking and washing, and for industrial and commercial processes. Global water demand is predicted to be 55 per cent higher in 2050 than it was in 2000.[54] As they get richer, people will choose to buy more food and put immense pressure on water supply. In 2009, a former UK chief scientific adviser, Professor Sir John Beddington, warned: 'We head into a perfect storm by 2030 ... Our food reserves are at a fifty-year low, but by 2030 we need to be producing 50 per cent more food. At the same time, we will need 50 per cent more energy, and 30 per cent more fresh water.'[55] Meeting this resource challenge will require a concerted effort on the part of industrialised and industrialising countries alike.

8. World disorder

Trotsky's warning that 'you may not be interested in war, but war is interested in you' applies even more strongly in the globalising age.

---

54   OECD Environmental Outlook, 2012
55   *The Guardian*, 18 March 2009

Britain has a large stake in, and a responsibility to uphold, a framework of international security that promotes trade and liberty. When international terrorist ideologies take hold across the world, revolutionary upheavals disrupt long-standing diplomatic alliances, and revisionist powers like Putin's Russia plot to undermine the framework itself, 'splendid isolation' is not viable.

Little exemplifies this more than the Liberal Democrats' policy of nuclear disarmament or their attempts to restrict arms sales to Israel, but the effects of refusing to face up to growing international instability are more dangerous and profound. Not only have Islamist terrorists once more carved out a base in a failed state from which to operate, the Russian threat has returned. Weak enough to feel insecure, but strong enough to pose a threat to the post-war geopolitical order, Russia assumes the proportions of a large, and disconcertingly nearby, rogue state. Its threat can be met, but the 'peace dividend' issued at the end of the Cold War has now been cancelled.

World trade depends on safe civilian air travel. The security measures taken at airports to thwart hijackers and terrorists are worth little when major powers export advanced anti-aircraft missiles to semi-trained irregular militia conducting a thinly disguised proxy war. International economic progress depends on being able to make investments at reasonable levels of political risk, and this ability is now under threat.

As Matthew d'Ancona has written, 'Goods, services and people are not the only things that cross borders with ease in the twenty-first century. There is also a global free market in the ideologies of hatred.'[56] Continuing political instability in Muslim countries will provide fertile ground for Islamist extremism for as long as the governments in those countries fail to meet their people's aspirations for freedom, opportunity and economic growth. The successful revolution in Tunisia has shown that progress is possible. There is nothing inherent in the region's culture that makes it impossible for democracy to take root. Liberty under law is, however, very hard to get right, and often requires several attempts to stick, as the French, Germans and Spanish will attest. Until it does, however, Britain will be exceptionally vulnerable to the consequences of that instability.

Years of misguided state-multiculturalist Labour policy contributed to a situation in which separatist communities, often of Muslims from the Indian subcontinent, became established but lived 'parallel lives'.[57] Within these, Islamist ideologies contemptuous of Western civilisation and democratic values found a ready audience. The Prime Minister robustly denounced this in his speech to the Munich Security Conference in 2011, arguing that the UK needed a stronger national identity to prevent people turning to all kinds of extremism:

> Under the doctrine of state multiculturalism, we have encouraged different cultures to live separate lives, apart from each other and apart from the mainstream. We've failed to provide a vision of society to which they feel they want to belong. We've even tolerated these segregated communities behaving in ways that run completely counter to our values.

The government has taken a tougher stance on groups promoting Islamist extremism. The once fashionable theory that violent extremists would be tackled by providing money and preferment to non-violent extremists is now rejected. Instead, the British values of parliamentary democracy, liberty, tolerance, equality and the rule of law are promoted.

Yet the difficulty in deporting so noxious an extremist as Abu Qatada, the 'Trojan horse' scandal in Birmingham, and the travel of a very small minority of British Muslims to Syria and Iraq to fight with ISIS, show there is considerably more still to be done. The fact

---

57   Ted Cantle, 'Community Cohesion: a report of the Independent Review Team', Home Office, 2001

that the problems relate to second-generation immigrants suggests a long-term failure of integration.

The challenge

So this is the sobering list of the immense challenges facing Britain, exacerbated by the global economic revolution: a country which is ageing without saving; persistent regional inequalities; excessive public spending and debt; fierce global competition; a technological revolution which has left state provision behind; mass migration; pressure on natural resources; and world disorder.

Disruptive though this recent wave of globalisation has been to world order, it is not entirely new. Indeed, its roots stretch back to the changes of global trade and technology of the nineteenth century and before. And the global economy has always experienced major changes and dislocations, with countries and empires rising and falling as the world changes around them. The challenge for each state, for each polity, is to adapt and respond, to ride the wave and not be sunk by it. The example of Argentina is instructive: one of the world's strongest and most promising economies at the start of the last century, it has steadily sunk down the league table of nations, despite the vast potential of its peoples and resources. It is a case study in political failure.

The scale of the challenges of globalisation reminds us that politics matters a great deal, and that it must deliver solutions. Government must respond to change, seize opportunities and counter threats. Politicians must lead and shape opinion. We cannot shrink from the task or belittle what must be done. It has fallen to Conservative governments in the past to chart a course for national renewal. Today we must draw on the principles that have served us in the past to shape a response that will steer Britain safely through the global storm.

Chapter 3

Values

Conservatism stands out in the philosophy that it adopts to respond to such multiple and simultaneous challenges. Unlike our political rivals, our instincts lead us to suspect they are not all linked by a single cause. By contrast, the leftist sees each problem as one of equality, and the state as the instrument by which it is to be solved, while the liberal insists that each issue stems from a lack of freedom, and posits the state's removal as the solution. Recent years have also seen a return, to use a term applied to anti-immigrant protectionist populists in the late nineteenth-century United States, of a 'nativist' style of politics to the UK. The nativist, now exemplified by UKIP, identifies problems as originating abroad, and aims to avoid them through autarky. The essence of conservatism is quite different: it rejects each of these grand theories, not just because each of them is wrong, but also because no grand theory can possibly cope with the complexity of the problems at hand.

'To be a conservative', Michael Oakeshott famously said, 'is to prefer the familiar to the unknown, to prefer the tried to the untried, fact to mystery, the actual to the possible, the limited to the unbounded, the near to the distant, the sufficient to the superabundant, the convenient to the perfect, present laughter to utopian bliss.'

Observations of this kind infuriate our political opponents. They drove a man as wise and courteous as John Stuart Mill to stoop to

insult us as 'being by the law of their existence the stupidest party'.[58]
Those who follow Mill, convinced of their theories, do not understand
that a Conservative attitude to the business of government is less a
plan to better the people by imposing a pattern of rules upon them
than a desire to allow them to retain, amid changing circumstances,
the pattern to which they are accustomed. Yet Conservatives are
not, in this respect, only traditionalists. Our mission is not limited
to standing with William F. Buckley, 'athwart history, yelling Stop',[59]
although when the country is heading for disaster this becomes the
most urgent Conservative duty. Even traditionalists agree that, as
important as it is to maintain our heritage:

> Conservatism cannot discharge its role simply by mouthing the slogans
> and battle cries of the past. Its business is to say what the application of
> these principles is to the present and to preach this application in the form
> of a concrete and practicable programme of government. There is there-
> fore no inconsistency in a Conservative describing himself as a reformer.[60]

Nor are we purely liberals. We do not always consider individual rights
to be 'trumps'[61] that serve to end discussion and command action.
Unlike liberals, for whom a commitment to free markets is a matter
of abstract principle, the value we place on free, competitive markets
is founded on the overwhelming evidence of history that individuals
make better economic decisions for themselves than when governments attempt to manage the economy, and that capitalism, rather
than state planning, has produced the prosperity we enjoy today.
And although our party has always been blessed by more than its
share of adventurers, those who take delight in overturning established patterns of authority, it is as content adhering to convention.

---

58 John Stuart Mill, *Considerations on Representative Government*, 1861
59 William F. Buckley, 'Our Mission Statement', *National Review*, 19 November 1955
60 Quintin Hogg, *The Case for Conservatism*, 1947
61 Ronald Dworkin, *Taking Rights Seriously*, 1977

The individualist instinct in conservatism co-exists with an appeal to the importance of social order. Its protection often demands greater resort to state power than the Whig principle of liberty under law would allow. Though it contains libertarians within it, we have never been – and should not be – a libertarian party. Conservatism has often been at it strongest when fulfilling the people's demands for security from crime and revolutionary upheaval, both of which destroy the individual security on which freedom depends. 'Liberty', warned Robert Peel, as he faced opposition to setting up the first modern police force, 'does not consist in having your home robbed by organised gangs of thieves.'[62]

The Conservative understands that there is a proper use of state power. The question is the purposes for which it is exercised, and how it is to be limited. As R. A. Butler noted, 'We have used the power of the state since Bolingbrook in the time of Queen Anne, long before Socialists were ever thought of, but we have always used it to foster and preserve individual freedom.'[63]

The notion of excessive or arbitrary state power is repellent to Conservatives, but so too is untempered liberalism. Conservatives could never contemplate a world in which every human want is unrestrained. In the twenty-first century in which the icy winds of global competition blow, in which the extraordinary freedom of modern technology also presents new dangers, and in which the very intensity of change makes the familiar seem a refuge, a creed which celebrates a lack of restraint is alien to the Conservative temperament. As Jesse Norman has written:

Extreme liberalism is now in crisis ... But, as Burke shows us, the individual is not simply a compendium of wants, human happiness is not

---

62 Letter as Home Secretary to the Prime Minister, the Duke of Wellington, 1828, *Peel's Papers* (ed. Parker), Vol II, p. 128, quoted in *Robert Peel*, Douglas Hurd, 2007, p. 10

63 Quoted by Paul Dean in 'Conservative Points of View', Conservative Political Centre, 1964, in *Political Ideologies*m 1984, p. 105

simply a matter of satisfying individual wants, and the purpose of politics is not to satisfy the interests of individuals living now: it is to preserve an evolving social order which meets the needs of generations past, present and future.[64]

Nor is there a need for a liberal party when, as R. A. Butler noted, 'all that is best in the Liberal tradition has long been absorbed into Tory philosophy'.[65] What has made us a single party, content to adhere at different times to figures as diverse as Keith Joseph and Lord Liverpool, or Lord Salisbury and Harold Macmillan, is an appreciation that political power is held in trust, and that those who for the time being hold it only ever entirely represent part of the tradition in whose name they exercise it. They are the section of the Conservative family that the circumstances of the time have pressed into service, but they do not have a monopoly on its wisdom.

The judgements of each generation of Conservatives emerge from the interplay of the timeless values that compose the party's tradition, which in turn derives its suppleness by acknowledging that the importance given to each value varies with circumstances. They provide a richer, and truer, conception of conservative thought than has often been acknowledged, even by Conservatism's defenders.

The Conservative principles that I have identified are nation, security, liberty, community, equality and opportunity. This selection is deliberately catholic: to reduce the party's tradition to a single principle, even one as important as liberty, is to misunderstand conservatism. In the remainder of the book I shall explore how each of these principles inspires specifically Conservative responses to the challenges of our age.

---

64 Jesse Norman, *Edmund Burke: The Visionary Who Invented Modern Politics*, 2013

65 '... belief in personal liberty, in the importance of the individual, in the virtue of property-owning, in free enterprise, in fair competition and in national unity.' B. Sewill, notes for R. A. Butler's speech at Luton Hoo, 21 June 1958, quoted in *Ideologies of Conservatism*, E. H. H. Green, 2002

Chapter 4

Nation

Labour pulled at the wires of the British constitution without knowing what they might disconnect. They endangered the fabric of the Union by devolving extensive power to Scotland but giving it little real fiscal autonomy and so no ability to exercise the responsibilities that come with it. They imposed the Lisbon Treaty on Britain, reneging on their promise to put it to a referendum. Tony Blair even accidentally abolished the office of Lord Chancellor in a Cabinet reshuffle and hurriedly had to reinstate it to avoid constitutional chaos. The contrast with the Conservative approach to constitutional change could not be greater.

Disraeli said that 'the Tory Party, unless it is a national party, is nothing'.[66] But we are not nationalists. Orwell drew the vital distinction between patriotism, 'devotion to a particular place and to a way of life', and nationalism, which is 'inseparable from the desire for power'.[67] A century after the outbreak of World War One, we should remember the destructive power of nationalism, and shudder that it is still causing conflict at Europe's borders. Conservatives should eschew the narrow appeal of nationalists and reject identity politics. As Orwell noted, 'no nationalist ever thinks, talks, or writes about

---

66 Speech at banquet of the National Union of Conservative and Constitutional Associations, Crystal Palace, 24 June 1872, cited in 'Mr. Disraeli at Sydenham', *The Times*, 25 June 1872, p. 7

67 George Orwell, 'Notes on Nationalism', 1945

anything except the superiority of his own power unit'.[68] Conservatives are proud of our country and know what makes Britain great, but are also practical about our national interest. At best, exceptionalism permits complacency about decline; at worst, it leads to isolation.

Preserving the Union of England, Scotland, Wales and Northern Ireland has, therefore, been core to the Conservative Party's belief. Indeed, we are, historically and formally, the Conservative and Unionist Party. That is why we argued that our shared history and geography allowed the United Kingdom to be more than the sum of its parts, that together, we formed one of the most powerful countries in the world, punching above our weight in international affairs, and that we prospered together and would each count for less were the country broken apart. Even Alex Salmond was forced to acknowledge an element of this truth: his 'independent' Scotland would retain the UK's monarchy and (he claims) its currency.

At the time of writing, the referendum on Scotland's independence has not been held. If Scotland votes 'Yes', it will be a shameful rebuke for Westminster politics, a serious embarrassment for the government and a shock to the economy, and it will damage the prestige of the UK. As unionists, the Conservative Party would be deeply saddened by such a decision.

But the UK will recover and prosper, while an independent Scotland, in the grip of a socialist utopian fantasy, living beyond its means, will face rising taxes, spending cuts and long-term decline. As David Smith has pointed out, for the past quarter of a century, 'even with a geographic share of oil revenues, and even in a period when North Sea production was at its peak, Scotland has run a bigger deficit than the whole of the UK'.[69] It has enjoyed higher public spending financed by UK taxpayers. After independence, that subsidy ends.

If divorce must happen, it is in everyone's interests that it is

68   Ibid.
69   *Sunday Times*, 7 September 2014

amicable, but it cannot be on Scotland's terms. They cannot be permitted to share the pound. They may choose to use the pound, rather as Zimbabwe uses the dollar, but they can have no control over it, because that would damage both economies. No currency union has succeeded without political union. Twenty years ago, in the so-called 'Velvet Divorce', Czechoslovakia divided to create the Czech Republic and Slovakia. The countries agreed to share the Czech Koruna. The different pace of economic development in the two new republics made it impossible. The currency union lasted for thirty-three days, and Slovakia now has the euro. Sharing the pound would damage the UK and Scotland alike.

Nor should MPs for Scottish constituencies be permitted to allow the formation of a UK government in the 2015 general election, since they will no longer be members of the UK Parliament after 'Independence Day'.

That Scottish nationalism arose with such force is a symptom of the lopsided nature of devolution in the UK. Though the Scottish government has broad powers to enact policy (by some measures wider than those granted to German *Länder* or Spanish 'autonomous communities'), it will not be responsible for raising money to pay for them until 2016, when a Scottish income tax will be introduced. This asymmetry precludes a proper debate on fiscal policy and the role of government, while providing nationalists with the ability to blame funding shortfalls on an 'English' government in Westminster.

The effects of this asymmetry provide an important lesson for the further devolution which, if Scotland has voted 'No', is now inevitable in that country and which, in turn, raises the question of what should happen in England. The well-known West Lothian question, which identifies that Scottish and Welsh MPs can vote on English matters, but English MPs cannot vote on Scottish or Welsh matters, will have to be solved. But so, too, should the remoteness of English government from the English people.

Under current constitutional arrangements, it is quite likely that a government could be elected to office with the support of Scottish and Welsh MPs, despite lacking majority support in England. When the reverse occurred it stimulated the growth of nationalist sentiment in Scotland that was only partially dampened by devolution. It is not hard to imagine a government with a majority derived from its strength outside England imposing taxes that would be borne disproportionately by English taxpayers to finance policies of which English voters disapproved. Such situations would provide fertile soil for an English nationalism every bit as destructive of the Union as the Scottish and Welsh kind. Preserving the Union – our country – therefore requires significant constitutional change.

A minimalist solution of 'English Votes for English Laws' has much to recommend it. It fits in with the British tradition of constitutional evolution where constitutional changes are made incrementally, and with minimal disturbance, and therefore with political practice, instead of imposing abstract theoretical models of political order at the expense of good government. It dispenses with the need to create a wholly new institution and provide salaries for a further set of politicians. It is immune from what might be called the 'Prussian Question', when one unit in a formally federal country exerts disproportionate influence over the others due to its sheer size, as Prussia did in Bismarck's Reich.

A more radical alternative would be a fully federal UK, in which an English Parliament, comparable to the Scottish, was set up (with the assemblies of Northern Ireland and Wales becoming similar parliaments). Such a scheme would see the federal government of the United Kingdom retaining responsibility for areas such as foreign affairs, defence, immigration, overall macroeconomic policy and international trade, while an English Parliament, like the Scottish from 2016, would be able to raise its own taxes. The boundaries of jurisdiction would be settled by the UK Supreme Court, as they currently are between London and Scotland.

Either solution would raise the possibility of an English majority, quite possibly Conservative, being at odds with a UK majority. A fully federal system would expose these differences more clearly: there could be a Labour Prime Minister of the UK and a Conservative First Minister of England. The question, then, is which is more likely to provide a focus for a now latent but potentially damaging English nationalism: an arrangement that continues to ignore English claims, or one that answers them. What is clear is that this is no longer only a Scottish, or for that matter, a Welsh or Northern Irish question. Disraeli's observation that 'I am a Conservative to preserve all that is good in our constitution, a Radical to remove all that is bad'[70] is the beginning of wisdom in this debate. We should no longer allow hot-headed nationalism to dominate it. A constitutional convention is needed to examine the issues.

One nation

When Disraeli spoke of 'one nation', he was describing of the division between rich and poor. Today, such divisions of wealth remain, if not as starkly as in the industrialising nineteenth century, and others exist too: divisions between people of different religions, ethnicities and different regions of the country. A modern Conservative government should rule in the interests of the whole country. Since the riots in Burnley and Oldham there have been increasing efforts to dismantle institutions and policies that lead to people living 'parallel lives' and to promote integration.

But a main source of divisiveness now is the financing of our welfare state, which is almost uniquely reliant on universal payments and lacks any element of individual social insurance. David Goodhart has written that fostering the solidarity needed to sustain support for the British welfare state requires restrictions on immigration much

---

70   Campaign speech at High Wycombe, 27 November 1832, cited *in Selected Speeches of the Late Right Honourable the Earl of Beaconsfield*, Vol. I, 1882

tougher than those currently in force.[71] As the recession deepened, calls for economic protectionism grew; Gordon Brown notoriously called for 'British jobs for British workers' and Ed Miliband divided companies into 'producers' and 'predators', explicitly identifying the former as British.[72] These arguments are really directed against globalisation, of which movements of people are a part. As Chapter 2 of this book has identified, there are genuine concerns about the scale of immigration to this country which must be addressed, but rather than seeking to put up barriers simply to protect universal non-contributory welfare benefits, the right approach, as set out below, is to manage migration, as well as reforming the welfare system to make it contributory.

Choosing prosperity requires radical changes to how the state helps people plan for retirement, insure against illness and get themselves out of unemployment. The principle that people should be helped to take responsibility for their own lives is a long-established Conservative belief. Radical reforms based on that principle are needed to escape the politics of envy and suspicion that characterises populism of the right and left. Later chapters will set out how such reforms in welfare and health pensions might be achieved.

The economic gap between London and its environs and the rest of the country presents a puzzle to economists. In principle, labour is cheaper in depressed regions of the country, and capital relatively scarce. The returns from employing that labour upon capital transferred to the area ought to be high, and should attract entrepreneurs to the area. Yet, the gap that opened up between London and the formerly industrial cities of the north of England, following the restructuring of the economy after the money to subsidise unprofitable industries ran out, has grown instead of closed. The recent recession accentuated the divide, because during Labour's

71 David Goodhart, *The British Dream: Successes and Failures of Post-War Immigration*, 2013
72 Speech to the Labour Party conference, 2013

period in office many of these areas had been propped up by constant flows of state largesse extracted from taxpayers based elsewhere. The problem here is not the fact of redistribution, but its method and unsustainability. Instead of using the boom years to stimulate an entrepreneurial revival in places like Newcastle and Liverpool, it directed flows of state money and expanded the public sector labour force, paying for what was intended to be a permanent expansion of the state with cyclical revenues.

The secret to London's success has been clustering.[73] It has attracted ambitious individuals to work and develop new businesses in finance, consulting, the law, advertising and new technology, to name just a few areas. The same phenomenon drives Silicon Valley or the manufacturing hub of Shenzhen. During the industrial revolution it drove the textile mills of Manchester and steel production of Sheffield, but far less of global importance has been able to take hold outside of London in recent decades. Important clusters have arisen in Aberdeen (petrochemicals) and Derby (engineering), but they remain relatively small-scale. The very real effects of this phenomenon have stimulated new interest in industrial policy, but government's record in picking the correct ones leaves a lot to be desired. Politics is inevitably swayed by electoral considerations, while exciting new sectors yet to emerge will likely escape their attention. Direct attempts to identify the 'industries of the future' are likely to leave taxpayers' money backing the white elephants of the past.

Rather, what is needed is the development of an enterprise-friendly environment. This cannot be limited to public spending on infrastructure, important though this may be. Successful entrepreneurial clusters depend, overall, on three things: products, investors and labour. The northern regions' fine universities produce thousands of intelligent and ambitious graduates every year, but many of them move south

---

73   See Michael Porter, 'Clusters and the New Economics of Competition', *Harvard Business Review*, November–December 1998

after graduating, rather than stay to develop the innovations in the life sciences or physics on which they have been working. Though some of this is due to the unavoidable pull of London, other factors are clearly at work. Possibly most important is the lack of capital and entrepreneurial activity: the proportion of income earned from profits in London is almost double that earned in Greater Manchester.[74]

Because of the extent of state-directed misallocation of capital that propped up unsustainable industries, the effects of whose collapse are still felt in northern regions, state action is justified by way of compensation. A radical solution would be to designate Britain's major cities outside London as large-scale enterprise zones, in which major tax incentives were allowed to stimulate investment. For instance, to attract capital, new investment in businesses, the bulk of whose activity would be based in the zone, could be exempted from capital gains tax for, say, twenty years, and new businesses could qualify for a large allowance to set against business rates. Measures such as these could both attract long-term capital and remove a significant obstacle to the survival of new businesses. The effects of a revival of enterprise in the birthplace of the industrial revolution could be extraordinary.

Many of Britain's cities could be strong engines of economic growth like Dusseldorf or Turin, or cities in states like Texas. Manchester, Liverpool, Leeds, Newcastle and Sheffield had global ambitions once. Labour anaesthetised them with state subsidy for failing industries and then by trapping them in dependency on the public sector. Conservative policies can foster the entrepreneurial culture that underpinned their glory.

Britain and Europe

Though geographically close to, and frequently politically involved in, the European continent, Britain is also a maritime nation that has

---

traded and settled across the seas. We retain a cultural and political affinity to Australia, New Zealand, Canada and the United States that the Continental land powers never did; we have a different legal system from those in Europe. NATO, rather than the Common Foreign and Security Policy, is our preferred institution for collective security. The ideal of European integration was born in the shadow of the Second World War, but 'ever closer union' is not, and will never be, the British destiny. Because we rightly – despite the calls from many businesses and, of course, the Liberal Democrats – did not join the euro, we were able to deal with the financial crisis more quickly and flexibly.

Despite the level of regulation, and the costs of net contributions to the EU, the overall economic benefits of Britain's current position, within the EU but outside of the eurozone, should not be underestimated. British companies have access to the largest single market anywhere in the world, and their access will increase as the transatlantic trade and investment partnership is negotiated. It is in Britain's interests for the EU's economies to reform, create jobs and promote growth. A British exit, particularly one on bad terms, would jeopardise access to that market and its economic benefits.

Since Britain held a referendum on European Community membership in 1975, the institution has changed dramatically. Then a club of nine, each with a veto over policy and chiefly focused on trade and tariffs, it has now expanded to twenty-eight. The majority of decisions in major areas of policy are now taken by 'qualified majority'. The areas over which the EU has a say have also expanded substantially, to include justice and home affairs, labour market regulation, foreign policy and even, through the European Banking Authority, banking regulation. The European Parliament repeatedly claims ever greater authority to decide on matters affecting the whole union. Even the name has changed: originally a limited 'European Economic Community', it is now the all-encompassing 'European Union'. Unlike in other countries, where the treaties enacting these changes have been put to the people in a referendum, the British people have had no say on this process since the original referendum in 1975. Indeed, no one under the age of fifty-seven has had a say at all.

In a landmark speech in January 2013, David Cameron committed the Conservative Party to holding a referendum on Britain's membership of the EU by 2017, should the party win the next election.[75] The referendum presents a vital opportunity not just to settle the question of Britain's membership, which has become a growing issue in our country, but to focus the EU's agenda on securing the reforms it needs. This is not merely to suit British interests. The EU remains uncompetitive, the pace of economic growth in the eurozone alarmingly sclerotic. Reform is needed for all EU member states. Because it will be preceded by a renegotiation, the Conservative Party's referendum pledge represents a powerful opportunity to secure change for everyone's benefit.

As the Prime Minister argued in his speech, we need an EU focused on restoring its members' economic competitiveness, one that pulls out all the stops to secure a full trade agreement with the United States, as well as negotiating better terms for trade with fast-growing emerging markets in India and China. The single market in services needs to be completed to drive growth and shake up somnolent and over-regulated industries. Rather than imposing yet more regulation, the European Commission should be focused on removing obstacles to entrepreneurship, such as the Working Time Directive, and promoting trade across the world. All this is essential if young people in Spain, Italy or Greece are ever to get good jobs. Between 1980 and 1998 average growth in the eurozone was just 2 per cent, lower than Australia, Canada, the USA and the UK. But from 1999 to 2012 the situation became even worse, with average growth in the eurozone of just 1.5 per cent. Average unemployment in the eurozone is 11.5 per cent; it is over 10 per cent in France, over 12 per cent in Italy,

25 per cent in Spain and over 26 per cent in Greece. The unemployment rate for young people across large parts of southern Europe is even higher.

Reform requires that governments across the EU implement the kinds of difficult economic measures that Britain enacted in the '80s, and Germany pushed through in the '90s. Spain's centre-right government has overcome large street protests and trade union opposition to make labour markets more flexible. Its reforms are starting to work: unemployment there has begun to fall.[76] Italy's Prime Minister's task is even tougher. Economists tasked with reforming the Italian labour market were assassinated as recently as 2002.[77] They need an EU that helps them reform, and is focused on removing regulations, not developing additional rules and obstructing overdue economic change.

A Conservative government would push such a reforming, outward-looking agenda, because the United Kingdom benefits from a prosperous, economically successful Europe, not one that is mired in arguments resulting from the eurozone crisis. An EU focused on prosperity for its citizens, determined to make the most of new technologies and the opportunities that globalisation provides is essential. As Angela Merkel has observed, the EU cannot continue being responsible for 50 per cent of the world's social spending while producing just 25 per cent of its GDP. The two need to be brought into balance by reforming labour markets, removing obstacles to entrepreneurship to raise output and providing public services more efficiently.

Conservatives want to see an EU that is reformed and ready to seize the opportunities for trade within and beyond its borders to the growing economies of Asia and Latin America, as well as with traditional continental markets in the United States. The case for change is made more urgent by continued economic underperformance that

---

76   'Iberian Dawn', *The Economist*, 2 August 2014
77   'Dangermen', *The Economist*, 18 February 2012

is creating social tensions even in the EU's original members: Germany now shares British concerns about benefit tourism.[78] These will get worse if southern Europe's economies do not reform. Recent increases in migration to the UK have been driven by arrivals from Portugal, Italy, Greece and Spain in search of work. Although allowing people to move to work in places where labour is needed is part of the purpose of the single market, the United Kingdom cannot function indefinitely as the EU's employer of last resort. As Boris Johnson has said, we need 'managed migration'.[79]

The Prime Minister has shown that a tough negotiating strategy can work. He secured a reduction in the EU budget. He vetoed an EU treaty that did not have adequate safeguards for Britain's interest and in particular the City of London. And the European Union Act 2011, which triggers an automatic referendum if it is proposed to transfer powers from Westminster to the EU, will ensure that a future government can never impose further integration without the consent of the British people. Labour's reneging on its promise to hold a referendum on the Lisbon Treaty – which further increased the areas on which the UK could be outvoted – was one of the most damaging acts in undermining trust in politics of modern times.

The Conservative agenda for reform in Europe should aim to create a more competitive, more economically free, and more successful European economy. As Boris Johnson described it:

> I want a Europe of opportunity, a cartel-busting, market-opening Europe, a Europe of mutual recognition where we get back to the sublime simplicity and wisdom of cassis de Dijon rather than the grinding mastication of harmonisation and job-destroying regulation; a Europe in which we truly take decisions at the level they need to be taken.[80]

---

78 'Germany considers capping child benefit for migrants', *Financial Times*, 27 August 2014
79 Speech at Bloomberg, 6 August 2014
80 Ibid.

Reform must allow for the possibility of a change of direction. If other countries want to integrate further, that is their choice, but there should be no obligation for Britain to join them in that process. A 'multi-speed' EU which commits all to 'ever closer union' would not be acceptable because it implies a shared destination that Britain would eventually be compelled to accept, only more slowly.

Reform must also protect the interests of the City of London, the financial capital of Europe, which is essential to British and European prosperity. We need to ensure that measures to expand the eurozone or protect the single currency do not provide opportunities for those envious of its success to strangle it in regulation. We must use robust mechanisms to prevent the City being subject to domination by the eurozone, such as the 'double majority' devised by Open Europe and adopted to prevent eurozone members outvoting the rest,[81] and conduct our European diplomacy at the very top of our game.

However, even with reform to reduce bureaucracy and regulation, the existence of a single market poses questions about our ability to control our own borders, since it requires companies and individuals from the different countries that compose it to be able to compete on equal terms.

To see why, observe what happened in Germany. Unlike Britain, Germany imposed transitional controls on immigration following the entry of eastern European countries. Though this prohibited eastern Europeans from being formally employed by German firms, it did not prevent self-employed individuals moving to Germany or, indeed, German firms subcontracting to Polish or Czech ones. When controls were lifted, eastern Europeans did not surge into Germany because so many of them were already there, albeit not as formal employees.

---

81   'Safeguarding the single market: How to achieve a balanced European Banking Authority', Open Europe, 2012

Ending controls allowed them to use the German welfare state, but it did not give them any new entitlement to participate in the German economy.

Reform is needed to alleviate the negative effects of free movement and help us manage migration flows from the rest of the EU. As the Prime Minister said, 'It is time for a new settlement which recognises that free movement is a central principle of the EU, but it cannot be a completely unqualified one.'[82]

First, there should be no entry for criminals. We should be allowed to deny entry to our country to people with criminal records. Other EU members would be able to bar our criminals, as we would theirs.

Second, there should be welfare responsibility. People who move countries to work should remain attached to their own welfare system until they have contributed enough not to be a burden on the society to which they have moved (each person would be given a transferrable 'pot' into which their contributions would go).

Third, we should transform our own welfare state to make it contribution-based, so as to promote incentives to work and ensure that our own citizens are equipped, through their education and training, to meet the needs of businesses which must compete in today's global economy.

Fourth, as the Prime Minister has suggested, EU countries should be permitted to slow full access to each other's labour markets if economic imbalances necessitate it to prevent excessive migration flows – for instance through caps on inflows above a certain annual level.

These reforms would address public concern and enable more balanced migration. They could be agreed by qualifying, not eliminating, one of the fundamental freedoms of the EU: the movement of labour. There is a trade-off between the various effects of the single market: the larger market for goods and services is inseparable from the larger labour market, which brings with it the effects of residency.

Article in the *Financial Times*, 26 November 2013

Getting the balance on labour movement right is a microcosm of the overall dilemma we face. The benefits from a reformed EU, focused on growth and prosperity, in which the single market functions to allow businesses across Europe to take advantage of this area of 500 million people, and with a GDP similar to that of the United States, are very large. The advantages of belonging to an inward-looking, over-regulated and slowly growing club, one that ignores the opportunities presented by fast growing and flexible emerging economics in favour of the preservation of outdated and rigid social democracy, are far fewer.

Exit would not be without significant risks. To gain access to the single market, British businesses would still have to abide by European regulations, but would lack representation in setting them. Like Switzerland and Norway, who must implement EU law without having a say on it, we would be standard takers, not standard setters. (The Swiss negotiate with the EU on each area of EU law individually, while the Norwegians have signed up to the whole single market.) We would no longer be required to make a contribution to the EU budget, but would have to pay a fee to access the single market instead. Where we are now an important conduit for English-speaking countries, with whom we have historic ties, who seek to conduct trade and diplomacy with Europe, we risk being bypassed if we are outside.

Our relationship with the United States, which sees the EU as a mechanism for preserving stability on the Continent and limiting Russian influence, would be affected. It is, furthermore, far from clear whether a British exit would be concluded on good terms. While it would be in Brussels's economic interest to arrange comprehensive free trade agreements with the UK on generous terms, the EU also has a strong interest in preventing itself from unravelling. The terms on which we would secure access to our nearest and largest market would not immediately be clear, and this uncertainty would itself be damaging. The City's position as the pre-eminent global financial centre would also be challenged. American banks are already reported to be making contingency plans to move operations to Dublin or Frankfurt.[83] Though similar fears were voiced that the City would lose business if Britain did not join the euro, and these proved to be misplaced, the danger this time is legal, not economic. EU financial regulations require financial products to be approved by its authorities. The question therefore becomes whether our most important industry is safer in or outside a reformed EU.

We will need to judge, at the referendum, whether the reforms to the EU that are secured, as well as the domestic economic reforms that other states carry out, are enough to bring these effects into the kind of balance we think is in the long term interests of the United Kingdom. We are not Liberal Democrats, because we do not see only the benefits of EU membership. We are not UKIP, because we do not see only the costs. If there is sufficient reform to the EU it will remain in our national interest to stay in. If we cannot secure satisfactory changes, especially in relation to immigration, we should be prepared to leave. Under a Conservative government, it is the public – in a referendum which will be held in less than three years' time – who will decide.

---

83 'US Banks Plan Ahead for UK Exit from EU', *Financial Times*, 17 August 2014

Chapter 5

Security

The security of the citizen is the first duty and primary function of government. People need security from criminals, terrorists, and international threats. They also need security from illness and misfortune. Furthermore, today's globalised economy puts increased pressure on personal finances. Conservatives believe in strong social institutions so that people can make decisions about how to prosper and foster opportunities for their children in a world where we are all subject to intense competitive pressure. We have long understood that this imposes a duty on government to ensure that our country possesses the means to ensure security. Today, security is no longer defined in its narrowest sense. Just as we cannot live beyond our financial means, we cannot live beyond our environmental means, either.

At first sight, Tony Blair's strong stance on foreign intervention and his 'tough on crime' rhetoric might suggest that Labour promoted security. But his government also passed the Human Rights Act and undermined public confidence in the criminal justice system through the early release of offenders. Ed Miliband's opportunistic opposition to military intervention in Syria, despite earlier assurances of support for the government, signalled that he intends to depart from what has, in general, been a responsible Labour stance in foreign policy. It would be deeply regrettable – and worrying – if such isolationism found its way into office. Indeed, few previous

British governments provide precedent for it. By contrast, the Prime Minister showed strong and resolute instincts in leading the intervention in Libya, which averted terrible massacres in Benghazi and Misrata. The Conservative Party must maintain that leadership today.

Britain's role in the world

Those who would like Britain to take a less high profile role in the world choose to classify her as a medium-sized power. This is a gross underestimate. By most measures we remain a major nation: we have the sixth largest GDP;[84] the fifth largest defence budget;[85] and we are second only to the United States in overseas aid spending.[86] We have considerable capabilities, and a consequent responsibility to use them to uphold international stability and promote progress. If defence and overseas aid spending are added together, the UK devotes $74 billion to international affairs, the third largest amount of money in the world after the United States ($631 billion) and China ($137 billion), but ahead of Russia ($68.8 billion), Saudi Arabia ($65 billion), France ($64 billion), Japan ($63 billion) and Germany ($58 billion).

This has remained the case despite the economic downturn and the need to deal with the deficit, which has meant cuts to Britain's armed forces. As operations in Afghanistan wind down, our defence spending is set to drop below NATO's recommended level,[87] though the growth of aid spending has allowed around a tenth of the aid budget (approximately £700 million each year)[88] to be spent on governance and security.

With the privilege of permanent membership of the UN Security Council comes a responsibility to 'do the hard work' of upholding the international security architecture. This means maintaining

---

84   World Bank, 2013
85   'The Military Balance', International Institute of Strategic Studies, 2013
86   OECD, Official Development Assistance ranking, 2012
87   *Financial Times*, 15 June 2014
88   DfID Annual Report and Accounts, 2013

strong and efficient armed forces and a diplomatic service tasked with operating the institutions of the international order in the interests of Britain and fellow democracies (not just mercantilist trade promotion). It also means continuing our work in international aid to build up the accountable, efficient and democratic institutions that provide people with freedom and the means to achieve prosperity.

It is a responsibility to which public and political opinion seems increasingly reluctant to face up. Since 1945, incomes in this country have increased fourfold,[89] trade has expanded immeasurably, and the ease of travel has opened it up to millions. This has been possible because there have been eight decades free of major international war. The left-wing conceit that poverty causes war is questionable. The reverse is all too true. War causes poverty through its destruction of people, property and hope, and the ability to plan for the future.[90]

Thomas Hobbes understood this most clearly. 'Covenants', he said, 'without the sword, are but words, and of no strength to secure a man at all.'[91] The establishment of order, not a retreat into pacifism, is necessary for the establishment of peace. If in domestic affairs, this requires an efficient police force, a strong system of justice, and effective punishment of criminals, abroad it demands that we contribute to an active foreign policy. The overreaction to the errors made in the prosecution of the Iraq War has produced a public mood across Britain and the United States where too much of the political class is unwilling to face up to this responsibility. It has retreated into a great shirk or denial, whose consequences are being felt in Ukraine and Iraq.

When the government took office, it could be forgiven for concentrating on domestic affairs. In 2010, the international environment appeared relatively benign. British troops had begun to withdraw

---

89 'Annex to The UK Recession in Context: What do three centuries of data tell us', Bank of England, 2009

90 See for instance Gary Haugen, *The Locust Effect*, 2003

91 Thomas Hobbes, *Leviathan*, 1651

from Iraq and were beginning to plan the winding down of their operations in Afghanistan. It seemed like the perfect time to order an aircraft carrier without being certain when the planes would be ready, and plan a foreign policy focused on the promotion of trade, while the nation licked the economic wounds inflicted upon it by Labour.

This judgement, reasonable at the time, has turned out to be wrong. The Arab revolutions of 2011 made a stability-first policy in the region untenable. Intervention in Libya was fully justified, but attention to building the institutions of a post-war state was insufficient. The low point of British policy was undoubtedly Ed Miliband's cynical manipulation of the parliamentary vote on military action in Syria, in which he secured parliamentary opposition by specious invocation of the entirely different situation of Iraq in 2003. Parliament demanded the right to vote on war and peace, which should be the prerogative of the executive, and then showed itself incapable of addressing those matters with the seriousness required. The return of Russian expansionism reinforces the need for change in Britain's national security activity to promote the alliances and democratic governments that are the surest bulwark of our security.

If the expansion of free government is best achieved by diplomatic and economic means, military intervention is necessary and justified to prevent and stop serious crimes against humanity. This is an old Conservative tradition. Michael Gove has traced the use of intervention to support democracy and prevent tyrannical abuse to 'the enlightened conservative response of past British statesmen', including Canning and Churchill, 'distinct from both the principle-free realpolitik of other conservatives and the utopian liberalism of the left'.[92] One of its most important modern advocates has of course been Tony Blair, whose speech in Chicago before NATO took military action in Kosovo remains true today:

92 'The Very British Roots of Neoconservatism and its Lessons for British Conservatives' in Irwin Stelzer (ed.), *The Neocon Reader*, 2004

We are all internationalists now, whether we like it or not. We cannot
refuse to participate in global markets if we want to prosper. We cannot ignore new political ideas in other counties if we want to innovate.
We cannot turn our backs on conflicts and the violation of human rights
within other countries if we want still to be secure.[93]

Together with our allies in NATO, and alongside countries such as
Australia, Canada, Japan and New Zealand, we, the world's democracies, must act together to preserve the international architecture
of global security, and resist attempts by tyrants and terrorists to
divide the community of democratic nations. If it necessarily falls
to the United States to assume global leadership of this mission, its
major allies must also do their part. Despite economic difficulties in
many ways more severe than ours, and exacerbated by their socialist President's perverse economic policies, France has demonstrated
impressive resolve in Mali, the Central African Republic and in supplying assistance to the Kurds. We need to exercise responsibility
and play our part once more.

Britain must have a clear, muscular vision of foreign policy. At
its core should be our national interest, but not petty nationalism.
Britain must protect and strive to further our interests and those of
other liberal democracies. We must defend our strategic and commercial interests and those of our allies, while not neglecting principles
such as the rule of law, representative government and human rights.
While we will not always be able to apply all these principles equally
– particularly when faced with the most powerful actors – they must
form the basis of our decision-making. And when we consider our
ability to project military force, the strength of our trade and commerce, our considerable soft power and our seat at the top table of
global power, we have an enormous ability and duty to shape global
opinion for the better.

---

93   Speech to the Chicago Economic Club, 24 April 1999

Environmental security

Responsibility for our security extends to the environment that sustains us and in which we all live. This responsibility is a profoundly conservative principle. As Margaret Thatcher, echoing Burke,[94] told the 1988 Conservative Party conference: 'no generation has a freehold on this Earth. We have but a life tenancy, and with a full repairing lease.'

Yet environmentalism made itself at home chiefly on the left. People forced to abandon Marxism after the collapse of the Soviet bloc found another reason to oppose capitalism: pursuit of wealth and economic growth would render the planet uninhabitable, or at least render the planet uninhabitable for the poor and prohibitively expensive to live in for the rich. They abandoned the best elements of Marxist thought, his obsession with improving living standards, and his belief in progress through technology and science, but kept the worst of the Marxists' methodology. Centralised state activity, planned by intelligent bureaucrats, would bring carbon emissions down, controlling people's behaviour when individuals' own decisions were insufficient to achieve the officials' ends.

But Red-Green environmentalism will fail because it goes against the grain of human nature. It has already failed internationally because countries did not trust each other to adhere to an agreement when their interests diverged. Poor countries sought to industrialise, not to be paid (occasionally by their former colonial oppressors) not to. In Britain, Labour – with Ed Miliband at the helm as Environment Secretary – designed decarbonisation policies that have imposed heavy costs on ordinary people struggling to make ends meet. Liberal Democrat energy secretaries have maintained the course. The Department of Energy and Climate Change estimated last year that carbon reduction policies currently add 17 per cent to household

---

94 'Society is indeed a contract ... a partnership not only between those who are living, but between those who are living, those who are dead, and those who are to be born', Edmund Burke, *Reflections on the Revolution in France*, 1790

electricity bills, and will have added 33 per cent by 2020 and 41 per cent in 2030.[95] British energy policy has managed to combine what the *Financial Times* has described as 'the inefficiency of state planning with the expense of private capital exacerbated by the fear that politicians will retrospectively change their minds'.[96]

Though state intervention can sometimes be justified as a response to market failure, rather more market failures in the energy industry derive from an excess of state intervention, not its shortage. Renewables ought to be part of the energy mix but it should not be government's job to dictate what proportion of our energy they generate, because subsidies for specific types of generation risk locking the UK into outdated technology. The same lessons apply to energy security. Before US shale gas production took off, the conventional wisdom[97] had been that the UK had lost out because it did not sign long-term contracts with its energy suppliers. But long-term contracts concluded in 2009 would have left us paying higher gas prices than we do today. Ill-advised subsidies have raised the cost of the electricity that will be produced by the Hinkley Point nuclear plant to £92.50 per MWh (compared to a market price of £55.05).[98] The UK's energy security position is good: most of our gas is either domestically produced or sourced from stable Norway. Since Britain is an island, it has good access to liquid natural gas from the global market. There may now be domestic potential for fracking, provided that it is undertaken in appropriate locations and with environmental safeguards, and the revenues could be channelled into a sovereign wealth fund.

The Red-Green policy consensus is technologically pessimistic, internationally naive and runs counter to an understanding of

---

95   Estimated impacts of energy and climate change policies on energy prices and bills, Department of Energy and Climate Change, 2013
96   'Britain's Energy Market needs Perestroika', *Financial Times*, 27 October 2013
97   Even the IoD argued for subsidies: 'Electricity Generation – Will the Lights Go Out?', *Big Picture*, December 2009
98   'Hinkley Point nuclear power contract "may be invalid"', BBC News Online, 6 May 2014

markets. The weight of the argument in the Stern Report[99] is that it is more economically efficient to use technology available now, to arrest the effects of carbon emissions before climate change's effects get worse, than to develop new technologies that will be able to address the problems more quickly. This is the standard Malthusian error, but where Thomas Malthus thought that agricultural technology could not improve swiftly enough to keep pace with population, the Red-Green consensus is convinced that technology cannot advance to keep pace with climate change. It appears related to the opposition to technological advance that is orthodoxy in the green movement. Left-wing greens dismiss what they term the 'technological fix',[100] because they are convinced that technology cannot correct the many problems they find in modern industrial society, but only postpone them until the inevitable reckoning. Human economic progress, however, *is* a matter of using resources ever more efficiently, and the free market under the rule of law is the best mechanism so far devised for persuading people to work in making both the frequent incremental improvement and occasional major breakthroughs required to do so. As Zac Goldsmith has argued:

Our defining challenge is to marry the environment with the market. In other words, we need to reform those elements of our economy that encourage us to damage, rather than nurture, the natural environment.

The great strength of the market is its unique ability to meet the economic needs of citizens. Its weakness is that it is blind to the value of the environment. Unrestrained, we will fish until seas are exhausted, drill until there is no more oil and pollute until the planet is destroyed.

But other than nature itself, the market is also the most powerful force for change that we have. The challenge we face is to find ways to price the

---

99   Nicholas Stern, 'The Economics of Climate Change', HM Treasury, 2006
100 For a discussion of orthodox green thought see Andrew Dobson, *Green Political Thought*, 2007

environment into our accounting system: to do business as if the earth mattered, and make it matter not just as a moral choice but as a commercial imperative.[101]

Green taxes can change behaviour, and in principle it makes sense to tax activities which are harmful. Revenue from environmentally related taxes (in current prices) has gradually increased over the past two decades, peaking at £43 billion in 2013. This is a relatively small but not insignificant proportion – 7.5 per cent – of the total tax take, equivalent to 2.7 per cent of GDP,[102] and despite the coalition agreement to 'increase the proportion of tax revenue accounted for by environmental taxes', it has remained broadly the same. However, green taxes such as air passenger duty, from which revenue has more than trebled over the last decade, are perceived to have added to people's tax burden. For green taxes to win public acceptance, they must clearly be offset by other tax reductions, not used as an easy justification to raise more revenue.

The insufficient application of capitalism to carbon emissions through a well-run carbon pricing system, or its emulation by means of a carbon tax, has held us back. An alternative to costly state-subsidised environmentalism exists. It is to move towards a system where the market is allowed to operate to reduce the amount of greenhouse gases required to travel, make goods and services and produce our food. Though basic research would be underfunded if the market were left entirely to its own devices, supplementing this with public research funding and scientific prizes would be far cheaper and yield much greater benefit than the central planning currently adopted. It would be tragic if it took the failure of international climate negotiations to demonstrate the folly of adopting expensive and inefficient solutions to a problem that

101 Zac Goldsmith, *The Constant Economy: How to Create a Stable Society*, 2009
102 ONS, UK Environmental Accounts, 2014

can best be met by technological advance and innovation. As Matt Ridley suggests, future technologies will produce carbon-free energy sources at lower cost:

> The way to choose which of these technologies to adopt is probably to enact a heavy carbon tax, and cut payroll taxes (national insurance in Britain) to the same extent. That would encourage employment and discourage carbon emissions. The way not to get there is to pick losers, like wind and biofuel, to reward speculators in carbon credits and to load the economy with rules, restrictions, subsidies, distortions and corruption.[103]

This approach has broader application to the other resource challenges that global economic development produces. Capitalism, backed by basic scientific research, has already worked extremely well in addressing what was thought in the 1970s to be the chief environmental problem: that we would run out of important resources. Not only have new mines been opened, and old ones used better, but due to other technological advances, minerals are also now used much more efficiently: cars for instance, are made of far less steel than they were, and are considerably more fuel efficient. A similar story can be told about food production: the green revolution vastly increased rice and wheat yields. Modern irrigation techniques allow arid areas to produce far more while abstracting less water. 'Lean and green' business represents a conservative attitude to the wise use of resources, the reduction of waste and greater efficiency.

While in some senses nature is priceless (as a later chapter will argue), we can in fact value an ecosystem's 'services', and it is where natural resources are not properly valued, for instance water, that they can become depleted. Bio-diversity offsets, or conservation credits, are a market means by which the damaging effects of

---

development can be mitigated, and the credits used to create new habitats which are at least as valuable as those lost.

We should turn our backs on Red-Green environmental policies, not the need to protect the environment. Blue-Green environmentalism embraces technology, progress, competition, the profit motive and what works. It goes with the grain of human nature and is true to Conservative principles. It is inherently optimistic, and it is essential to our environmental security.

Personal security

These global aspects of security mean little if our personal lives are insecure. Personal security is a matter of retaining one's liberty, one's ability to plan and make decisions about one's own life.

The left-wing approach to this is too often to deny the personal responsibility of criminals and imagine that impersonal social factors, rather than individual moral decisions and character, can explain crime, while its attitude to the latter is to rely on the impersonal instruments of the state.

Conservatives, by contrast, insist that criminals are individually responsible for the crimes they commit and believe that this has to be a central part of criminal justice policy, even when other policy measures can rehabilitate prisoners and help them reintegrate into society.

The physical security of one's person and property from attack or fraud is essential, but it has never been sufficient. Our needs extend further, to security from the shocks and misfortunes that life deals us. After the global financial crisis, and following a severe economic downturn when real incomes have fallen, people are more than ever seeking such security in their lives. Personal security against economic and other misfortune is best assured by the widest possible distribution of property which is protected from the unpredictable effects of political populism.

Despite significant reductions in crime across the West over the last two decades, there is more to be done. We have one of the most expensive criminal justice systems in the world, where effective prevention has been the poor relation in policy, and resources have historically ended up in the part of the system that comes into play when things go wrong – especially prisons. Re-offending accounts for half of all crime.

The best way to address crime is to prevent it occurring in the first place. Targeted crime prevention measures, paid for by results, should tackle drug and alcohol abuse and other social problems underlying a significant proportion of crime. But when offending occurs, it should always have consequences. The first instances of wrongdoing, very often nuisance or anti-social behaviour, must be dealt with effectively. Too often the state behaves like a bad parent, neglectful in repeatedly tolerating bad behaviour, then inevitably harsh. Failure to set clear rules and boundaries from the start, to deal with transgression swiftly and to prevent escalation, simply encourages offenders to flow through the criminal justice system until they are handed down a custodial sentence.

The agenda developed in the Conservative Party's policy paper 'Prisons with a Purpose'[104] represented a decisive and positive departure from the stale debate which suggested that the only choice was between more prison or less of it. In place of this one-dimensional approach was an agenda to break the cycle of crime. The government has implemented part of the 'Rehabilitation Revolution' which the paper set out, including payment by results to reduce re-offending and – for the first time – support for offenders on short-term sentences leaving prison. Now we must implement this agenda in full. 'Honesty in sentencing' requires sentences that specify a minimum and maximum term of incarceration be introduced, so that prisoners earn their release, rather than being released automatically at

---

104 'Prisons with a Purpose', Conservative Party Green Paper No. 5, 2008

or before the halfway point of their sentence. Except for the most serious offenders, we should replace the centralised prison system with local prison and rehabilitation trusts, paid for by results to reduce re-offending and answering – along with the probation service – to elected police and justice commissioners, as they should be re-designated. These commissioners should also assume responsibility for 'blue light' emergency services, which could become increasingly integrated at the local level.

Technological and justice innovation should allow us to move on from a binary choice between custodial or community sentences. Satellite tracking of offenders can already allow sophisticated curfews and protect the public, yet we have been slow to exploit its potential. In place of high-cost Victorian local jails, in which little is done to rehabilitate offenders on short-term custodial sentences, the private sector should build low-cost detention centres where offenders would attend intensive courses in the evenings, be curfewed at night and work under constant electronic supervision during the day. New units should be established in conjunction with the armed forces to train suitable young offenders for military service, as happens for instance in Indiana's 'Future Soldier' programme.

The Conservative reforms to improve the accountability of policing have – despite controversy – been one of our boldest and most important steps, but trust in the police remains too low, and after a series of debilitating incidents it is clear that police leadership must be strengthened. The government has promoted direct entry into higher police ranks, but we need to go further. The time has come to introduce an officer cadre in the police, as we have in the armed forces, including graduate bursaries for bright school leavers to go to university, followed by a 'short service' career commitment (in the army a short service commission is for a minimum of three and a maximum of eight years).

Despite reductions in spending on police and criminal justice, crime has continued to fall. This success should highlight the importance of a Conservative approach which focuses on outcomes, not how much is spent on services. Money is wasted if the roots of criminal behaviour are not addressed, police officers are not deployed efficiently, or offenders are not rehabilitated. Being right on crime means being smart on crime, not wasting resources that we no longer have, passing laws we do not need or indulging in populist rhetoric that does not deliver.

Security through ownership

Security goes beyond protection from crime. It is equally a matter of being able to deal with economic volatility from a position of stability. The Conservative principle is that nothing is more important to this than the ownership of property. In this respect, Ronald Reagan's warning about inflation – 'as violent as a mugger, as frightening as an armed robber and as deadly as a hit man'[105] – applies as much to inflation in property as in goods and services. Indeed, excessive property inflation is as an evil as great as the price inflation which destroyed jobs in the 1970s – and it should be seen as such, not celebrated or wished for. Its most serious effect is that it makes it too difficult for people to own their own homes. In the more expensive parts of the country, rates of ownership are falling, and by the 2011 census, a majority of Londoners had come to rent, rather than own, their own homes.[106] That is a trend which Conservatives should want to reverse. Rates of home ownership are higher elsewhere; the Chancellor's 'help to buy' initiative has enabled more than 48,000 people to own property, almost all first-time buyers and outside the capital.[107]

There is still a great fissure between social and private housing that raises social barriers that we should want to break down. There

---

105 'Inflation's Back', *The Economist*, 22 May 2008
106 ONS, 'A Century of Home Ownership and Renting in England and Wales', 19 April 2013
107 HM Treasury, 2 September 2014

will always be a place for good-quality social housing in Britain, but a third of social housing tenants are in work yet cannot afford to buy a home. High property prices feed through to higher rents, with the result that 95 per cent of the money spent by the government on housing is taken up by the housing benefits bill, which now costs £26 billion a year, with only 5 per cent invested in bricks and mortar.[108] We are spending public money in a way that maintains dependency on state provision rather than enables ladders out of it, that pays rents to private landlords but does not generate personal ownership.

Radical new measures to increase home ownership are needed. Shared ownership schemes have put property ownership within the reach of many who could not otherwise afford it. They could be boosted by creating financial incentives to invest in new shared ownership schemes. Less than 1 per cent of UK financial institutions' property portfolio is invested in the residential sector, compared with 47 per cent in the Netherlands, 21 per cent in the United States and 15 per cent in France.[109]

We should also allow social tenants to convert rent payments into a type of mortgage so that they begin to build a share of the ownership of the property, allowing them to realise their share once a certain threshold has been met. If the property was sold, the social provider would keep its share to enable it to build future social housing. This new 'right to own' could effect a powerful transformation from social tenancy towards home ownership. It would combine the power of the Thatcherite 'right to buy' with the Burkean requirement to preserve opportunities for the next generation.

Cheap money is one of the causes of the high price of houses, but we clearly do need to build more. Lack of housing supply remains a serious problem, particularly in the south. However, simply relaxing

108 'Building a Better Britain', Royal Institute of British Architects, 2014
109 'Institutional Attitudes to Investment in UK Residential Property', Investment Property Fund, June 2012

planning controls which have protected the countryside would be a foolish libertarian solution, not a Conservative one. The government was right to abolish top-down regional housing targets and instead give local councils the power and responsibility to plan. We need to take this principle forward and apply Conservative principles. We must not return to the bad old days of diktat and housing targets which do not deliver.

Neighbourhood planning shows real promise, allowing local communities to take control of decisions about where houses are built and receive a share of the benefits. It should be strengthened by making the rules that govern it less prescriptive and giving neighbourhood communities more powers. We should also give neighbourhood planning more support, rather as support has been given to those who wish to form new schools.

Major new developments such as garden cities could have an important role in providing new homes, but unsustainable new towns should not be imposed without local consent. It is the huge uplift in development land prices, which randomly benefits landowners, that is a principal cause of inflated prices, reflecting the excess of demand over supply. A system of community land auctions could be a market-led solution to the problem.[110] This release of land could enable an expansion of self-built homes, which account for 38 per cent of new homes in France and 30 per cent in Sweden, compared to less than 8 per cent in the UK.[111]

Security for the family

Families, too, are a vital source of security in any civilised society. Families nurture us and provide us with love and support. They are a source of social stability. This has been difficult territory for

---

110 See Tim Leunig, 'Community Land Auctions', CentreForum, 2011
111 'Build It Yourself? Understanding the changing landscape of the UK self-build market', University of York Centre for Housing Policy, 2013

Conservatives in recent years. How do we reconcile a traditional Conservative belief in the value of the institution of marriage with the liberal instinct not to judge how people lead their lives? Today, we recognise that modern conservatism ought to be about supporting all types of family: this is the generous Conservative instinct. That is why we supported gay marriage. As Andrew Sullivan argued so cogently in *Virtually Normal*,[112]

> Perhaps surprisingly ... one of the strongest arguments for gay marriage
> is a conservative one ... Conservatives should not balk at the apparent
> radicalism of the change involved ... The introduction of gay marriage
> would not be some sort of leap in the dark, a massive societal risk ... As
> it has become more acceptable for homosexuals to acknowledge their love
> and commitments publicly, more and more have committed themselves
> to one another for life in full view of their families and friends. A law
> institutionalising gay marriage would merely reinforce a healthy trend.
> Burkean conservatives should warm to the idea.

This argument was echoed by David Cameron, at the Conservative Party conference in 2011:

> I say: yes, it's about equality, but it's also about something else: com-
> mitment. Conservatives believe in the ties that bind us; that society is
> stronger when we make vows to each other and support each other. So I
> don't support gay marriage despite being a Conservative. I support gay
> marriage because I'm a Conservative.

Strong families are, if anything, becoming more important, because they help people support each other amid greater economic volatility. Among the kinds of care best received in families is the care we get from our parents when growing up, and the care we provide for our

---

112 1995

parents as we get old. Yet economic circumstances are such that too many parents, especially mothers, unless they earn very high salaries or are fortunate enough to have members of their extended family available close by, find that work does not pay enough to cover the cost of good childcare. They are forced to put their careers on hold, or not pursue them to the extent that they would wish, for instance by working part-time instead of full-time. This is a dilemma that, in the social arrangements that exist in today's Britain, men face far less frequently than women. It also contributes to a gender pay gap that is still far too large, both because women who take time out of employment gain less experience at work, and because they have to catch up after years spent working part-time or out of the labour force altogether. In 2012, the most recent year for which figures are available, the gender pay gap in the UK was 4.9 per cent between the ages of twenty-five and thirty-four, but 18.6 per cent between the ages of thirty-five and fourty-four. In Sweden, where childcare is much more widely available, it increases from 10 per cent to 17.5 per cent.[113] Before peak child-rearing age, UK earnings are more equal than in Sweden, but inequality between men's and women's earnings increases as people get older.

The government's childcare reforms, making it easier to pay a relative or friend to help with childcare without requiring that they register with OFSTED, and also making it easier for schools to provide nurseries, will help. A long-term solution would be to integrate childcare provision into the social security reforms proposed below.

Social security

A system which offers people unconditional benefits blunts the incentive to work, so the money by which the benefits are supposed to be funded will never be raised. Iain Duncan Smith is making great

---

113 'Gender pay gap in unadjusted form by age', Eurostat, 2012

strides against the immediate moral hazard that applies to working people. Perverse incentives in the housing benefit system have
been weakened. A single unemployed person with no children used
to be entitled to enough money to pay for a median one-bedroom
flat in the borough in which they resided. Were this system still in
place, someone living in central London would have to earn at least
an £65,000 a year to pass the credit check required to rent the same
property.[114] A stronger disincentive to work is difficult to imagine.
Imposing a cap on the total benefits that a family can receive has
further strengthened the incentive to work. These reforms may help
to explain why unemployment has fallen so quickly. Universal Credit
will, when it is implemented, eliminate still more perverse incentives that have crept into the benefits system.

Much more radical steps need to be taken, however, to address
the longer-term problems with social security, and in particular the
costs of healthcare and state pensions. These will, under current
arrangements, be imposed on people starting their working lives.
Previous generations trusted the system and paid their taxes, but
did not provide enough for their old age. Loading such costs on
future generations, including people who are not yet alive, is not
only immoral, it is also inefficient.

A pay-as-you-go social security system finds itself on the wrong
side of compound interest. Instead of putting money aside now and
investing it for the future, it borrows it, and imposes the burden of
paying the interest back upon its beneficiaries' children, making the
process horrifically expensive. The UK basic state pension currently
entitles a person to £5,876 per year. It would cost around £174,000
for a 65-year-old to obtain an annuity for that amount. Yet building
up a pension pot of that size over a lifetime is not inconceivable.[115]

---

114 For instance, 80 per cent of the median rent for a one-bedroom flat in Westminster
     would require an income of £52,000 – the median would therefore require £65,000
     (Westminster Council, Affordable Rent Statement, 2011); rents have risen since then
115 Though in practice people would invest different amounts, depending on their rate of income

A one-off sum of £5,000, invested to return a real rate of 3 per cent per annum over forty-five years, would yield £192,000. As around one million people reach adulthood in the UK every year,[116] providing each person in the UK with such a pot, to be invested by a state pension fund, would cost taxpayers £5 billion annually. This could be funded through savings in welfare, including restricting payments like winter fuel and free television licences to pensioners in need.

Other countries use this model: Ireland had established a similar scheme through its National Pension Reserve Fund system but was forced by the EU to use the accumulated money to bail out its banks.[117] Though not prohibitively expensive, and relatively easy to phase in, such a system does not, on its own, create sufficient incentive to work and spend. A system where the state provided generous top-ups to individual accounts within the fund, up to a certain level, would encourage this behaviour.[118] People would be free to add further savings of their own to these accounts. These principles would extend George Osborne's liberalisation of the pensions system that freed people from having to buy an annuity on retirement.

The same principles could be used to finance healthcare. Since risks to health may be divided into those related to age, those randomly distributed, and health risks associated with smoking, drinking and other forms of lifestyle, an alternative to a pay-as-you-go system can be envisaged. The former two kinds of risks may be financed through a health savings account system, as used in Singapore. There, a significant proportion of workers' income is diverted to individual health savings accounts rather than general taxation, and most of this money is invested by Singapore's Central Provident Fund to pay for Singaporeans' care as they age, with some diverted to insurance

---

116 Office for National Statistics, Mid Year Population Estimates Summary for the UK, 2013
117 'Irish Pension Fund to be tapped for €12.5 billion', *Financial Times*, 29 November 2010. The pension fund has now been converted into a sovereign wealth fund.
118 Michael Johnson of the Centre for Policy Studies develops a system on this 'matched savings' basis in 'Putting The Saver First: Catalysing a Savings Culture', CPS, 2012

schemes to address shortfalls in the system.[119] As a separate matter, so-called 'sin taxes' on, for example, tobacco, could then be used to generate funds to pay for the health costs of smoking. In a Singapore-like system, they could be used to fund insurance payments for treatment for smokers not covered directly by the health savings accounts.

The NHS could be financed in this way. Healthcare trusts could charge the health savings accounts and insurance schemes for the treatments they provided without requiring the intergenerational wealth transfers on which the NHS currently depends. Further ideas to reform the NHS are set out in Chapter 8. This chapter, on security, ends with this assertion: our personal financial security cannot be assured by taxing future generations beyond their means to pay, irrespective of what we contribute. Conservative principles require us to re-order our public provision so that responsibility is rewarded and saving is encouraged. We cannot go on spending today and sending the bill to our children.

---

119 W. von Elff, T. Massaro Y. O. Voo and R. Ziegenbein, 'Medical savings accounts: a core feature of Singapore's health care system', *European Journal of Health Economics*, 2002

Chapter 6

Liberty

Labour have little understanding of the British tradition of liberty under the law. They sought to supplant it with a confused tangle of entitlements that they wrongly describe as human rights. Edmund Burke described our liberties as 'an entailed inheritance derived to us from our forefathers, and to be transmitted to our posterity as an estate specially belonging to the people of this kingdom, without any reference whatever to any other more general or prior right'.[120]

These liberties are specific immunities from interference by other people and the state; they are protections from other people's power, not grants of a means to satisfy individual desires.

Left-wing entitlement rights are self-centred, peremptory demands that the state should make all of us provide, usually through our taxes, for what someone claims is their need. Liberty rights, in contrast, allow people to live together and get on with their lives without interference. The rights culture, devoid of responsibility, that grew up under Labour reduces freedom rather than enhancing it: it puts sensible people in fear of making reasonable decisions because they are afraid that someone will claim violation of an ill-defined right which is all too likely to be upheld by an authority.

Entitlement rights proliferate: the UN Declaration on Human Rights ranks a 'right to periodic holidays with pay' alongside

---

120 Burke, op. cit.

fundamental freedoms of speech and against arbitrary arrest. The rights 'contagion', as Dominic Raab has described it,[121] accelerated after the passing of the Human Rights Act in 1998. The Act brings into British law a form of jurisprudence quite alien to our judicial tradition, in which rights are seen as entitlements somehow belonging to individuals rather than devices by which the citizen can secure liberty and fair treatment from the state. It has produced a flurry of litigation in which courts have been put in the position of deciding questions that are more properly political, such as whether prisoners should be denied the vote. Perhaps worst of all, the very concept of human rights has been devalued in popular esteem.

We need have no quarrel with the rights set out in the European Convention of Human Rights. They were, after all, heavily influenced by British jurists. But in the hands of the European Court of Human Rights they have taken on a meaning of their own. One of the most egregious examples is the Article 8.1, the right to a family life. As written in the Convention, it is impossible to take exception to it: 'Everyone has the right to respect for his private and family life, his home and his correspondence.'

It conveys a meaning similar to the Fourth Amendment of the American Constitution: protection from one's home being seized, or spouses separated by a racist government, or correspondence seized by a spy agency without good cause. It was not intended to prevent criminals using the fact that they were married to escape deportation. The Strasbourg Court has gone further, inventing new rights that do not even exist in the Convention at all, such as a prisoners' right to vote.

We now have a Supreme Court that is perfectly capable of upholding human rights. There is no longer any reason to allow appeal offshore. Two objections are often raised to 'denouncing' (that is, leaving) the European Court of Human Rights. The first, that it would

---

121 Dominic Raab, *The Assault on Liberty*, 2009

require us to leave the European Union, is untrue. The second, that it would send the wrong signal to countries like Russia, is hard to take seriously when that country has just invaded another member of the Council of Europe, Ukraine. Neither objection should therefore prevent us from withdrawing from the European Court and reclaiming rights.

Responsibility

We should also pass a British Bill of Rights and Responsibilities to replace the Human Rights Act. Rights cannot exist without responsibilities. In order to consider people free and moral agents, we need to be able to attribute to them responsibility for their actions. To treat them otherwise, to ascribe blame for their mistakes or crimes to a generalised 'society', is to believe them incapable of liberty. None of this should prevent us from feeling compassion for people due to the circumstances in which they find themselves, or from assisting them out of trouble. Helping people towards a situation where they can make responsible decisions is one of the most important instincts behind compassionate conservatism: it underpins the 'Rehabilitation Revolution' in the criminal justice system and the progressive Conservative agenda for public service reform. When we enable people to take responsibility, we enhance their freedom and dignity. When the state takes away responsibility, it absolves individuals of accountability for their actions and cuts away freedom.

This freedom is just as important in the economic sphere. Conservatives are dismayed by the growth of regulation, not just because it undermines the competitiveness of business, but because it interferes with freedom and responsible decision-making. Many attempts have been made to reduce the burden of regulation. But only if we allow individuals to exercise their discretion and judgement, trusting people to act responsibly (while holding them to account for their actions), will we succeed in reducing the state's propensity to set rules for conduct.

Profit is good

Profit-making is to many on the left merely a necessary evil. No left-ist list of entitlements ever includes a person's a right to the profits from his or her own work. They have come to accept that, without the efficiency of the market economy, they would not be able to afford the expensive social programmes their philosophy demands. Yet they very easily choke on the notion of profit, which is funda-mental to capitalism and a free society.

The Conservative philosophy is different. We recognise the profit motive as one of the instincts that drives human beings to work hard, to innovate and to build businesses that can transform the world. As Enoch Powell argued:

> The politician's duty ... is not to rush around trying to supplant the profit
> motive, either by coaxing others or by trying to do the job himself ... It is
> to find out ... what it is that is stopping the profit motive from working ...
> Quite often the blockage will turn out to be some interference or series of
> interferences for which he himself or his predecessor are responsible.[122]

The left's attitude to commerce is like a farmer's attitude to his cows: businesses can be treated well, certainly – regarded with affection, even – but exist, in the end, to be milked and, ultimately, slaugh-tered. That businesses actually do something useful, or pleasurable, for which their customers freely choose to pay, does not form part of the leftist's assessment.

The amazing improvements in our standard of living created by capitalist production, from necessities like food and healthcare, to clothes and means of travel, to the arts and entertainment, that have advanced and been brought to the masses thanks to the profit motive and the disciplined force of market competition, are discounted. Suc-cessful businesspeople are instead seen as fortunate beneficiaries

---

122 John Wood (ed.), *A Nation Not Afraid: The Thinking of Enoch Powell*, 1965, quoted in E.
     H. H. Green, *Ideologies of Conservatism*, 2002

of factors 'arbitrary from a moral point of view'[123] who must repay society for their good fortune by supplying the state with revenue.

This shamefully underestimates the contribution that businesses make to society. They provide employment and opportunities to millions. The products and services they sell improve the lives of billions more. When Adam Smith noted that it was not from 'the benevolence of the butcher, the brewer, or the baker, that we can expect our dinner, but from their regard to their own interest',[124] the capitalist market economy was in its infancy. Since then it has produced products and applied technologies of which he could not even have conceived to better the welfare of mankind. It is capitalism and the profit motive, not left-wing economic policy, that have powered the growth of economies and east Asia. As China and India have abandoned socialism, they have begun to catch up on decades of growth on which they missed out.

But while profit is good, greed is not. With great wealth comes great moral obligation to others. Despite shining examples, the spirit of philanthropy that infuses the United States has not entirely found its way to the UK, perhaps because of our historically high rates of taxation. As these are reduced, a compact should be made: when the state confiscates less, society should expect more.

And profit is only good if secured fairly. Private or public monopoly can result in the exploitation of consumers. Theodore Roosevelt famously held that 'the mercilessness of private commercial warfare must be curbed'.[125] The 26th President challenged his own Republican Party and big business over 'predatory wealth ... the wealth accumulated on a giant scale by all forms of iniquity, ranging from the oppression of wageworkers to unfair and unwholesome methods of crushing out competition'.[126]

---

123 To use a phrase popularised by the influential social democratic philosopher John Rawls in his *Theory of Justice*, 1971
124 Adam Smith, *The Wealth of Nations*, 1776
125 Essay in *The Sewanee Review*, August 1894
126 The President's Message to Congress on Worker's Compensation, 31 January 1908

A Conservative Prime Minister, too, once spoke of 'the unacceptable face of capitalism'.[127] Conservatives should stand as firmly against unethical business and monopoly as we do for the virtue of profit. This ground must not be ceded to the left, who will use it to assault business itself. Indeed, Roosevelt's phrase has been twisted by Ed Miliband to mount a wider attack on business today. This is dealt with further in Chapter 10.

Low taxes

Conservatives recognise taxation as a necessity, not a virtue: the state performs important functions and these have to be funded, but we do not think we can spend other people's money better than they can themselves. As Margaret Thatcher said, 'There is no such thing as public money, only taxpayers' money.'[128] Taxes, not profits, are the necessary evil. They are always and everywhere an infringement of liberty. Taxes consist in the state taking people's money away under threat of force, to use it for its purposes instead of theirs. Furthermore, taxation involves the government, and not the people who hire you or trade with you, deciding how much of it you get to keep. The left see this as advantage; Conservatives do not. Though taxation is necessary, its level and its effects should be kept to a minimum.

We need to cut spending and limit government so that we can reduce the burden of taxation. There is no more powerful way to extend people's liberty than to confiscate less of their money. The priority for a Conservative Party that seeks to govern for one nation must be to cut taxes for those on lower and middle incomes. When Theodore Roosevelt proposed his 'square deal' for working people, he warned of the dangers of 'a government primarily for the benefit

---

127 Edward Heath, speaking in the House of Commons on the Lonrho affair, May 1973. He added that 'one should not suggest that the whole of British industry consists of practices of this kind'

128 Speech to the Conservative Party conference, 1983

of one class instead of a government for the benefit of the people as a whole'.[129] Conservative priorities should reflect this injunction.

In fact, tax reductions to help the poorest and those on average incomes have rightly been this government's priority. Increasing the personal allowance to £10,000 has meant a typical tax cut of £705, helping over 25 million people, while over 3 million on the lowest incomes will now pay no income tax at all. Someone working full-time on the minimum wage will have had their income tax bill cut in half. The government has also frozen fuel duty, meaning that families are saving £360 on petrol if they fill up their car once a week, and has enabled council tax to be frozen for four years running. The government also cancelled Labour's proposed increase in national insurance contributions immediately on coming into office. This tax on jobs should be a focus for further reductions.

But we also need to simplify taxes. Proponents of almost every particular special interest delight in devising tax incentives to promote their view of virtue and render what they conceive of as vice expensive, although an increase in the number of the virtuous erodes the tax base. More pernicious are taxes designed to favour particular economic interests or industries. They have the effect of channelling economic rents to those favoured by the detail of the levy. As it is, in general, established interests that command the political power to influence the tax code act as a barrier to innovation. Accordingly, the tax incentives proposed in this book are as general as possible: to invest, to save and to work. Precisely what work is done, enterprise invested in, or project saved up for, is left in the hands of investors, savers and workers. The absurd legal battle undertaken to determine whether or not Jaffa Cakes were classified as cakes or biscuits is but one example of the irrationality produced by complex tax codes favoured by special interests.

Furthermore, any tax imposes what is known as a 'deadweight

129 Speech to farmers at the New York State Agricultural Association, Syracuse, New York, 7 September 1903

loss' to the economy. Its creation makes certain activities, otherwise profitable, too expensive to be worth pursuing, and thus no tax can be imposed that only redistributes income, without reducing output below what it would otherwise have been. Meanwhile, discrete income tax thresholds create strong disincentives to work at the margin where the thresholds kick in.

The rich – rightly – pay the lion's share of taxes. The top 1 per cent of earners now contribute a record 29.8 per cent of all income tax, and the top 16 per cent of earners pay 67 per cent. But there is a danger of increasing the highest rates of tax in a way that is counterproductive and may actually reduce revenue. Gordon Brown did this for nakedly political reasons, introducing a 50p tax rate for the highest earners, which the government has rightly reduced to 45p. As George Osborne said:

> It is a completely phoney conception of fairness that you stick with a tax rate you know raises no money, that you know drives away jobs and investment, that you know weakens the economy, just to say you've kicked the rich. The people who pay the price for that are not the rich but the poor looking for work.[130]

If the evidence is that restoring the highest rate of income tax to 40p would raise revenue, it would be dogmatic and self-defeating to oppose it.

Populist political pressure has created other distortions. As tax-free allowances have increased, rightly taking more poor people out of tax altogether, countervailing measures have ensured that this does not at all reduce the total amount of tax paid by higher rate and 45p rate taxpayers. This practice, begun by Gordon Brown, has generated a perverse schedule of effective marginal tax rates that increases and decreases with income in a manner devoid of all rational pattern.

The consequence is that millions more taxpayers who earn more

---

130 Speech to the Conservative Party conference, October 2012

than the average but are far from rich have been drawn into the higher rate net. When the Conservative Chancellor Nigel Lawson cut the top rate of tax to 40p in 1988, just one in twenty taxpayers – some 1.35 million – were affected. By 2010, there were 3 million workers paying 40 per cent tax, while today there are 4.4 million and this will rise to more than 6 million in 2015 because the threshold rate – at earnings over £41,450 a year – will not increase in line with inflation.[131] The 40p rate is now invoked at levels of earnings where someone's net income would exceed the household benefit cap by only around £5,000.

Double taxation is also particularly resented, as for instance inheritance tax, which confiscates assets on a person's death that have been saved with income that has already been taxed. The Conservative manifesto in 2010 pledged to increase the inheritance tax threshold to £1 million, but this has been blocked by the Liberal Democrats, who, with their proposed confiscatory mansion tax, have a very different view of the right to own and retain assets. The Prime Minister has indicated that a majority Conservative government would raise the threshold:

> Would I like to go further in future? Yes I would. I believe in people being able to pass things down through the generations and onto our children. It builds a stronger society.
>
> Inheritance tax should only really be paid by the rich. It shouldn't be paid by those people who have worked hard and saved and bought a family house.
>
> The ambition is still there, I would like to go further. It's something we'll have to address in our election manifesto.[132]

The tax system should be as unintrusive, straightforward and neutral

---

131 *Daily Mail*, 10 March 2014
132 *Daily Telegraph*, 24 March 2014

as possible. Lower, simpler and flatter taxes are essential for our country's economic success and our citizens' liberty.

Quiet government

The Conservative belief in freedom is born of realism. It begins with the proposition that government officials and politicians are no better, and no worse, than the rest of us. They have the same instincts, capacities and flaws as the people. Unlike the left, Conservatives in government don't presume to be wiser than the citizens they govern. We believe that when people are free, they make better decisions, and that the more we trust them to make good decisions, the more they trust themselves to do so. Our instinct is to mistrust experts convinced that they have 'the' solution to intractable social problems, because people are too diverse and their circumstances too varied for a single solution to apply. It is much better, where we can, to limit ourselves to making sure that people have the tools, so that they can get the job done themselves.

In 1843, Jeremy Bentham set out his general rule that good government should 'be quiet' and 'stand out of my sunshine':

> With few exceptions, and those not very considerable ones, the attainment of the maximum of enjoyment will be most effectually secured by leaving each individual to pursue his own maximum of enjoyment, in proportion as he is in possession of the means ... security and freedom are all that industry requires.[133]

In the twenty-first century and the age of 24/7 media, it may seem ambitious to ask that frenetic government should be 'quiet'. But

---

133 Jeremy Bentham, *The Works of Jeremy Bentham, Vol. 3: Usury, Political Economy, Equity, Parliamentary Reform*, 1843. The Service of Communion in the Book of Common Prayer 1662 includes a prayer for the Queen 'that under her we may be godly and quietly governed'

Conservatives should recognise Bentham's plea for governments to do only what is necessary so as to maximise individual security, freedom and enjoyment.

There are many other reasons why Conservatives should continue to question the role and shape of government itself. If the technological revolution referred to in Chapter 2 is to be applied to government and the public sector, new skills will be needed to effect the transformation. If power is devolved, as Chapters 4 and 7 propose, central government will no longer need to be so big. If taxes are to be reduced, as this chapter proposes, spending must be reduced, too. If healthcare and education are to be personalised, as later chapters will propose, the role of government will change fundamentally.

Whitehall operates to a nineteenth-century model when we face 21st-century problems. It is bureaucratic and slow. Paper is still transported in ministerial boxes when the rest of the world has gone digital. Departments set up fiefdoms and fight with each other when problems require holistic approaches. Civil servants answer to ministers but are not appointed by them, meaning that ultimately they answer to no one. There are too many departments, too many ministers and too few expert advisers. It is hard to bring in people with outside experience into government. Whitehall lacks commercial acumen and skills, with the result that major projects are frequently costly – very costly – disasters. The only surprise is that it has taken so long for politicians to realise that reform is needed.

To make the changes which Britain requires will require changes to government itself. Francis Maude's reforms have made an important start. The government's Efficiency and Reform programme has saved £14.3 billion in just the last year through more efficient administration, including a reduction in the size of the civil service by 16 per cent, reformed civil service pensions, improved commercial procurement, the digitalisation of services, and better management of major projects.[134] The number of quangos has been reduced by a third. Extended Ministerial Offices now allow ministers to recruit more direct support, including from outsiders, as happens in Australia and Canada. A Contestable Policy Fund has occasionally permitted ministers to go outside the civil service for advice.

The next Conservative government should go further. It should be far easier to bring in outside talent, including policy and commercial experts, across Whitehall. Much more policy-making should be made contestable, so that the resource of think tanks and academic institutions is better used. We should sharpen the accountability of permanent secretaries to ministers, for instance as they do in New Zealand, reduce the number of ministers and government departments, and strengthen financial control across Whitehall. As power is truly localised, less should be done at the centre. We should have a smaller and more highly trained and incentivised core civil service, as they do in Singapore. Pay should be related to performance and delivery. A chief of staff with senior ministerial rank should run No. 10, with the equivalent status of the White House's chief of staff. A chief executive of Whitehall, recruited from industry, should also report directly to the Prime Minister. Sir Humphrey should be quietly retired to his club in St James's, and a new, business-like regime, fit for the modern world, brought in.

---

134 'Government unveils £14.3 billion of savings for 2013 to 2014', Cabinet Office, 10 June 2014

Chapter 7

Community

Margaret Thatcher's conservatism, like Ronald Reagan's, came to be seen more as nineteenth-century liberalism, its primary focus on freedom and the individual. One leading historian of the party even concluded that 'as the Conservative [twentieth] Century came to an end, it seemed that even if the Conservative Party had survived, conservatism had not'.[135] But Mrs Thatcher's much misquoted phrase that 'there is no such thing as society' created a false perception of today's party. As David Willetts, who has promoted the idea of 'civic conservatism', has argued:

> There are two strands to modern conservatism. On the one hand there is the commitment to the free market – with its appeals to the individual, to initiative, to enterprise and to freedom. On the other hand there is the trust in community, with its appeals to deference, to convention and to authority.
>
> Some commentators believe that these represent two fundamentally incompatible views of the world, and that free market *arrivistes* have taken over the party of deference and authority. In reality, both approaches can be traced right back to the origins of Conservatism.[136]

The Conservative belief in community is rooted both in our understanding of human nature and our suspicion of the state. People

---

135 E. H. H. Green, *Ideologies of Conservatism*, 2002
136 'Modern Conservatism', *The Political Quarterly*, Vol. 63, No. 4, October–December 1992

naturally want to associate with others and identify themselves not individually but as part of a group. Burke wrote of the love we have for the 'little platoon' to which each of us belong in society. It was on this rich and historic seam of conservatism that David Cameron drew when he promoted the 'Big Society':

> We know instinctively that the state is often too inhuman, monolithic and clumsy to tackle our deepest social problems. We know that the best ideas come from the ground up, not the top down. We know that when you give people and communities more power over their lives, more power to come together and work together to make life better – great things happen.[137]

The Big Society came to be seen more narrowly, as a cipher for volunteering, while the left inevitably suspected that it was a cover for public spending cuts and the dismantling of the welfare state. Both attacks were wrong. In fact, the Big Society was a big idea – 'a deep and serious reform agenda to take power away from politicians and give it to people', to use the Prime Minister's words[138] – and included a radical localism agenda that amounted to much more than the promotion of charitable work.

The left have never understood organic communities, instinctively preferring centralisation, direction and a hatred of difference that looks to them like inequality. They have come to like certain charities – those that promote left-wing ideas and ceaselessly call for higher public spending and more state intervention – rather as they suddenly saw the opportunity to promote socialism through the European Union. But, overall, Labour's preference is for big government.

That is why Labour has never been serious about localism. When they did consider devolving power, it was to regions, many of which did not actually exist. Presented as a plan to devolve government,

137 Speech at the launch of the Big Society programme, 18 May 2010
138 Ibid.

regional assemblies would in fact have sucked power up from district and county councils. Labour has never liked the shires, probably because the historic shires do not like them.

By contrast, the government embarked upon its localism agenda with purpose. The Localism Act abolished regional development agencies, replacing them with local enterprise partnerships. It also abolished regional planning, introduced neighbourhood planning and allowed for referendums on mayors. At the same time, unelected and invisible police authorities were abolished and directly elected police and crime commissioners introduced. More recently, city deals across the country have seen new powers and resources devolved from central government.

The agenda represented a policy *volte face* from the 1980s, when the Conservative government, appalled by the behaviour of left-wing councils and police authorities which let down local communities, decided that the only solution was to emasculate them. This action merely culminated a trend which had occurred throughout the twentieth century: central government grew, becoming ever more remote from the people it was supposed to serve. Once powerful civic institutions, including the great city governments of Victorian Birmingham and Manchester, lost sway as their powers were centralised in Whitehall. Magnificent city and town halls stood like museums, echoes of an age where mayors and aldermen exercised real power in their municipalities.

Yet, despite progress in devolving power, English government remains excessively centralised. Some areas of government, such as welfare, have been completely immune from any localist tendency. Others have seen reversals to decentralisation. Ministers have used the Planning Inspectorate, which should in fact be abolished, to drive housing numbers which were meant to be determined by councils following the abolition of regional targets.

A programme to decentralise power should not just mean transferring it to local government. The right approach is to return power to the 'lowest' possible level: where we can, to individuals – for instance by extending choice in public services or giving people control over personal budgets, such as in relation to care. We can go much further, as other chapters set out, with budgets for healthcare and education.

Where individual power is not appropriate, communities can be enabled, for instance through neighbourhood planning, which is showing real promise. When people have control, they act responsibly, rather than opposing development. In Thame, for example, residents voted for a neighbourhood plan that included the development of 775 new houses.[139] Communities have also been given new powers to control local assets, which they have used, for instance, to save village pubs. Now we can go much further. In Rotterdam, a 'Neighbourhood Takes Charge' programme has seen communities given real control over the allocation of community policing resources, boosting civic participation. We should allow neighbourhoods to take charge here.

In many areas of policy, it will be appropriate for elected bodies to take decisions. We rightly created new elected offices, mayors and police and crime commissioners, but failed to see how vested and political interests would conspire to frustrate the change. Yet the success of the Mayor of London shows that elected individuals can answer the demand for local accountability when properly empowered.

The answer is to push again for localism, and this time push more effectively and with conviction. Directly elected mayors in Liverpool and Bristol have provided a focus for local, responsible politics. The other great cities of England also deserve London-style mayors controlling the elements of urban government: transport, housing, city-wide planning, certain social services in the areas over which they have control. Outside cities, we should directly elect council leaders, or replace them with elected mayors.

---

139 'Two more neighbourhood plans make the grade', Local Government Planning Portal, http://www.planningportal.gov.uk/general/news/stories/2013/may13/090513/09052013_2

As with Scotland, however, powers to raise significant revenue have not been devolved sufficiently. Local taxes – council tax and business rates – account for less than 10 per cent of total UK tax revenue, and there is no direct linkage between money raised locally and the spending of local authorities, due to the centrally controlled system of local government finance.[140] Mayors should become responsible for more local revenue raising. Cities need to be free to build their own identities and pursue their own plans without having to justify themselves to Whitehall. The right to set business rates and keep its revenues are obvious targets for devolution.

Police and crime commissioners had a difficult start, partly as a result of an attempt by the Liberal Democrats to sabotage the policy – true to form and despite the coalition agreement – by demanding that the first elections were held in November. But good local commissioners are already making a difference in their communities. The right step is to give them more powers, over probation and local criminal justice services, to allow a holistic approach to the reduction of crime and re-offending, and ensure a justice system responsive to local communities. Making them police and justice commissioners would maximise the value of the new office and increase its appeal. Police force amalgamations, ostensibly to save money, would be the wrong way forward: they would take policing further away from local communities. Savings can be made from more effective force collaboration. If anything, stronger national policing, for instance through the creation of the National Crime Agency, should allow for smaller forces which are more closely connected to local communities. This would enable the role of police and crime (or justice) commissioners to be taken by directly elected mayors, as in London.

Localism should be core to the Conservative belief that individuals and communities should be strengthened, given more power and choice, and incentivised to act responsibly. The 'dark star' of central

---

140 'A tax system fit for the future: an economic perspective on tax reform', PwC, 2014

government exercises a powerful but frequently malign gravitational pull. Power which should be personal or civic should not be held in Whitehall through inertia or vested interest. The Big Society may no longer be a fashionable phrase, but its Conservative ideas are timeless and vital.

Conservation and heritage

The Conservative emphasis on community and responsibility is reflected in our attitude to our heritage. Conservatives recognise the importance of markets in allocating resources, and, usually, prefer market mechanisms to central planning. Chapter 5 set out a Conservative approach to protecting the environment, harnessing the power of the market to incentivise the right behaviours. But, unlike classical liberals, we treat markets as a means, not an end. To be a Conservative is to believe, with Edmund Burke, that our heritage should be conserved and passed on to the next generation. Conservatives should, after all, believe in conservation.

Included in the heritage to conserve is our cultural patrimony, and Britain's reputation as a place renowned for its cultural innovation. Unlike classical liberals, for whom everything is reduced to its economic value. Conservatives believe in the intrinsic importance of art and cultural expression. It forms part of what we are, and ought to continue to be in the future. It has developed with our country, its landscape, its history and architecture. It includes the English language but spreads beyond an artificial notion of 'British values' and is part of our contribution to creating Western civilisation. Our traditions of liberty and democracy are only a part of this heritage.

It is impossible to talk about Britishness without talking about the value of our heritage, urban and rural, architectural and pastoral. The Conservative attachment to the countryside, in particular, should be deep and immutable. From Keats's evocation of the 'stubble-plains' and 'river-sallows' of autumn, to Vaughan Williams' meditations in his Fantasia; from Constable's great pastoral landscapes to Hardy's 'realistic dream country' of rural Wessex, our landscape has inspired our artists to expressions of natural beauty which speak to what it is to be English. Like '*La France Profonde*', 'Deep England' draws on a connection with the natural world which is almost spiritual. It is a pity that while visitors to our country see this link so clearly, instantly identifying our natural heritage as an integral part of national culture and identity, we are ourselves so slow to appreciate it.

We must beware of a kind of cold Conservatism, a cousin to unbridled liberalism, that limits an appreciation of national or community assets or institutions to their economic value. Though these things may have an economic or instrumental value, that is hardly their point. We don't only value the armed forces because they protect us, nor the monarchy because of its constitutional role. Rather, they constitute part of our identity and the fabric of society. Conservatives identify with these assets and institutions, and seek to protect them by instinct. Indeed, it is one of the characteristics that make us Conservatives, and it reveals why others, such as liberals who may otherwise share much of our appreciation for liberty and opportunity, are not.

Compassionate Conservatism

The Conservative belief in community should also be reflected in a generosity of spirit. We do not believe in state largesse, or that compassion can be measured by how much public money is spent. Across government, we should be sceptical of pledges to meet arbitrarily set targets to spend at particular levels, being more interested in the effectiveness of spending and its outcomes. But that should not blind us to the obligations which wealthy nations have to the poorest in the world. It is through trade and economic development, fostered through property rights and the rule of law, that underdeveloped countries will grow. But while poverty persists, it brings with it millions of victims who need clean water, food and medical aid. Tuberculosis, for instance, easily treatable and curable and nearly beaten in the West (though now making a dangerous comeback in drug-resistant forms) still kills 1.3 million people a year worldwide. Without the intervention of Western nations, there is no commercial incentive for pharmaceutical companies to develop a vaccine or new drugs to tackle a disease of the poor. State action is needed to address such market failure. The help that countries like Britain has provided, including through international agencies like the Global Fund, has saved millions of lives. We should be proud of what we have done through our aid programme to bring relief to the poorest in the world. Such action is realistic about British interests in an interconnected world, but it is also profoundly moral. Compassionate conservatism should be the hallmark of our party today.

Chapter 8

Equality

Some might raise an eyebrow at equality being identified as a Conservative value. To the extent that they do, it is testament to the effectiveness with which Conservatism's opponents have appropriated the value. Our disagreement with the left is first, not about equality's importance but about the thing to be equalised, and second, the direction in which equalisation is to take place.

The left understands equality as people being assigned 'equal shares' of the resources of society, under decisions made by the state. What we consider fundamental rights, they see as items to be distributed equally. For them, the distribution of rights and the distribution of income are two aspects of the same phenomenon. But when rights are conceived, as Chapter 8 argued that they should be, as immunities rather than entitlements, they can be held by everyone without denying them to anyone else. One person's right to freedom of speech does not restrict another's; nor does a criminal's right to a fair trial deny his victim the right that justice be done, since a fair trial of a guilty defendant should result in his conviction.

Equality is often conflated with imposing ethnic and gender quotas, yet equality is about treating individuals equally, irrespective of these characteristics. Merit and application should be the only factors limiting someone's potential attainment, not, for example, their gender, race or sexuality. Conservatives must demand that barriers limiting opportunity are removed – for instance by strengthening childcare for all to support women at work. Our commitment through equality ought to be to an equal liberty; attempting to fill quotas instead defines individuals by their characteristics and risks those favoured by the system being seen as tokens rather than appreciated for their worth. The logic of quotas is to seek a 'Goldilocks proportion' – neither too few nor too many – of each specified characteristic. Quotas demand a bureaucratic superstructure and run counter to a liberal principle of treating people individually and assessing them on their character and talent. Equality protects individuality; quotas undermine it.

We used to say that while the left believed in equality of outcome, Conservatives rejected it in favour of equality of opportunity, but in truth we believe in maximising opportunity, not equalising it. This is because opportunity can just as easily be equalised by taking opportunities away from those who have many as securing them for those who have few: as in the Office for Fair Access in higher education, which seeks to make it harder for some young people to go to university because of their parents' social background.

This misunderstanding of equality engenders centralist over-regulation in public services, giving managers, not patients and parents, control of vital public services. Rather than reducing inequality, it increases it by creating a situation where only the rich can afford to escape the mechanisms of control and levelling down.

In this area Conservatives seek to give the poor an equality of power over essential services that is currently enjoyed only by the wealthy. We should achieve this by levelling up: enabling the poor to exercise consumer power over education and healthcare currently at the disposal of the relatively affluent.

Equality of power

To be poor is to be subject to assessment, means-testing, investigation and accounting for one's actions. It is constantly to apply for things, and be in a position where a bureaucrat decides your fate.

It is to be subject to remote and complex procedures that have the ostensible aim of determining fairness.

These tests are multiplied because taxpayer's money is scarce, and people want to be assured that it is used on the deserving. The effect is to sap initiative and imply to people that by default they are criminals and fraudsters. It inculcates values contrary to responsibility. It infantilises the recipients of help.

The British state has long worked this way. You 'apply' for schools for your children; you 'apply' through your GP for medical treatment, and you wait to see if you pass the tests developed more as disguised rationing than as ways to provide children with the best education or patients with the best care. This rationing of public services has led to staggering and persistent levels of inequality in our society. As Fraser Nelson has argued so eloquently, a baby born in Liverpool is likely to die five years before one born in SW1 at the same time. This gap is as wide as the gap in life expectancy between blacks and whites in the United States.[141]

By any standards, this leftist method for reducing inequality has failed. Centralised bureaucracies, commanded to meet vast quantities of targets, and subject to detailed inspection by regulators determined to extinguish the 'postcode lottery' produced the opposite. Doctors and nurses, instead of being allowed to care for their patients, are subject to so much control and performance management that they are in danger of becoming automata. It is this culture of top-down administration that produced the scandal at the Mid Staffordshire NHS Trust, where between 400 and 1,200 people died unnecessarily between 2005 and 2008[142] amid what the subsequent public inquiry described as the 'appalling suffering of many patients'.[143]

---

141 Fraser Nelson, 'We have no reason to feel smug about America's troubles', *Daily Telegraph*, 22 August 2014
142 'NHS targets "may have led to 1,200 deaths" in Mid-Staffordshire', *Daily Telegraph*, 18 March 2009
143 Robert Francis QC, Report of the Mid Staffordshire NHS Foundation Trust Public Inquiry, 2013

Faith that our system of public services is 'fair' is so great that it can blind those who should be holding an institution to account for its faults, while any critic or proponent of reform is attacked. Labour persistently attacks the Conservatives for wishing to undermine the NHS, yet the last Labour government ignored eighty-one requests for a public inquiry into the Mid Staffordshire tragedy to uncover and address systemic failings.[144] When *The Guardian* reported a recent study which ranked the NHS the best health system out of eleven industrialised countries, it noted – apparently oblivious to the irony – that 'the only serious black mark against the NHS was its poor record in keeping people alive'.[145]

In response to Mid Staffordshire, the Health Secretary, Jeremy Hunt, has prioritised patient safety, publishing a league table of key safety indicators across all major hospitals (the first of any country to do so), introducing a tougher inspection regime and demanding a focus on patient care. But if incidents like this revealed an issue of culture, they also raise questions about accountability.

Medical staff have been monitored from above, by what – until this government took office – was a fast-growing class of hospital and NHS managers. The government's NHS reorganisation has removed 19,000 administrators. But the number of managers is an inevitable outgrowth of the apparatus of bureaucratic control that has its origins in Aneurin Bevan's desire that the sound of a dropped bedpan in Tredegar should reverberate around the Palace of Westminster. It is the logical conclusion of the 'top-down egalitarianism' pioneered by Sidney and Beatrice Webb. Labour believed, and the evidence of centralisation during their last period in office indicates that they continue to believe, that if only the right information can get to the right people in charge, large bureaucracies can be administered

---

144 The Mid Staffordshire NHS Foundation Trust Public Inquiry Vol. 1, 6 February 2013, p. 9; Hansard, 13 February 2013, col.735W

145 Denis Campbell and Nicholas Watt, 'NHS comes top in healthcare survey', *The Guardian*, 17 June 2014

efficiently and in a way that provides equal treatment. In reality it secures only what George Will has called 'equality in the form of equal dependence of more and more people for more and more things on government'.[146]

The reverse idea, that public services should be accountable to the members of the public who use them, should not be an original thought. Conservative administrations have made repeated inroads into the centralist education complex, thereby increasing opportunity for the disadvantaged. Now it is healthcare where there is the greatest need for reform: to make the NHS responsive to patients and thereby stimulate the competition that will keep costs down while improving the service people receive.

Competition works because it gives consumers power over their suppliers, who do not need to be told to maintain a standard of service by managers or through detailed, centrally directed targets, because they fear losing business. The forces of competition work powerfully both in the supply of essential services, like food, and in complex, technical consumer-facing industries where safety is hugely important, such as air travel. Effective regulation and law are sufficient to keep travel safe and food supply reliable. Centrally directed control of the food supply, in the form of rationing by the peacetime Attlee government, was abolished thanks to Conservative pressure in 1954. It is unimaginable today. So is the idea that well-known independent high street opticians would not exist, yet a service with little choice of glasses was once provided by the NHS alone.

The central myth attached to the current method of administering the NHS is that it provides healthcare to all, free at the point of use. Yet this is untrue. In fact, the NHS uses queues, in the form of waits for treatment; rationing, through National Institute for Health and Clinical Excellence (NICE) guidance (and administrators to oversee it); and charges, for instance for prescriptions, dental care and eye

---

146 George Will, 'The Case for Conservatism', *Washington Post*, 31 May 2007

tests, to limit costs. As Andrew Haldenby, Director of Reform, has pointed out, 'Charges have been part of the English NHS since 1951. In the early years of the NHS, they raised a greater proportion of the budget than they do now.'[147] Polish immigrants were reported to be so dissatisfied with NHS primary care that they have set up private health clinics across England where they pay for the prompt and efficient care to which they are accustomed.[148]

Without radical reform, the use of these expedients will continue or increase, and there will be pressure to spend more. Even if funding is kept to a constant share of GDP, the NHS in England claims that the health budget will be £30 billion short each year in seven years' time.[149] Tax rises to meet this are out of the question. Nor can other budgets be cut much further to make up the difference: the NHS has already been exempted, due to the ring-fencing of its budget, from the large spending cuts to which other government departments have had to adapt.

The government is increasing spending on the NHS by £12.7 billion in this parliament.[150] This is funding new treatments like the £1.16 billion Cancer Drugs Fund, which has already helped more than 55,000 people,[151] and has enabled the recruitment of 7,000 more doctors and 4,000 more nurses. Activity has increased: 35,000 extra people are being treated for cancer, 70,000 more are being diagnosed and treated for dementia, and overall 850,000 more operations are being performed annually. Fewer people are waiting more than eighteen weeks for an operation. When Labour left office, 21,908 were waiting more than a year for their operation. By July 2014 this had fallen to 510 people.

The question is how a future government will be able to deliver

---

147 Andrew Haldenby, 'Can we ignore NHS charges any longer?', The King's Fund blog, 20 August 2014

148 'Another kind of health tourism', The Economist, 8 June 2013

149 'A new settlement for health and social care', The King's Fund, 2014

150 HM Treasury, Budget 2013, p. 69

151 Department of Health press release, 28 August 2014

improving healthcare, given the constraints on resources and rising demand. Labour is said to be flirting with the idea of a hypothecated tax rise to fund extra spending on the NHS.[152] The Director of the Institute for Public Policy Research (IPPR) has proposed a one-percentage-point increase in one of the national insurance rates, ring-fenced for the NHS, which would raise £4 billion. He claims this 'could be popular'.[153] Yet the tax burden on families is already too high, and the additional revenue raised would be insufficient in the long term. Others propose additional NHS charges, and these have been introduced in other European countries, but with multiple exemptions for charges in England they would be likely to raise even less revenue.[154]

Instead, we should focus on the system itself. A continuing near monopoly of health supply, despite the entry of some independent providers, limits potential productivity gains. Under Tony Blair, Labour endorsed the principles of competition within the NHS, despite initially having abolished GP fundholding and reversed the internal market (the reforms introduced by John Major's government under which providers purchased care). They also allowed the private sector to provide care to NHS patients. Labour's perennial attack that the Conservative Party seeks the 'privatisation' of the NHS is therefore as hypocritical as it is false. Alan Milburn, a former Labour Health Secretary, said: 'When I introduced private sector providers, some claimed it would be the end of the health service as we had known it. In fact, they strengthened it.'[155] The NHS does not have to *provide* all care itself to guarantee *access* to care. Healthcare can be – and is – provided within the NHS system, free at the point of use, by independent providers, including mutuals or the

---

152 *Financial Times*, 29 August 2014

153 Nick Pearce, 'An NHS tax is needed to keep the NHS free to all at the point of need', The King's Fund blog, 14 August 2014

154 Andrew Haldenby, 'Can we ignore NHS charges any longer?', The King's Fund blog, 20 August 2014

155 *Daily Telegraph*, 15 June 2011

private sector. Indeed, GPs are not employed by the NHS; most are self-employed but are contracted to it.

This government has replaced Labour's primary care trusts with GP-led clinical commissioning groups, with the aim of making the services they commission more sensitive to patients' needs. However, the patient still has no real power.

The inefficiency of the centralist model increases the need for rationing and queues. Its bureaucracy and arbitrariness reinforce health inequality: articulate and well-educated members of the middle class are likely to have much better success at disputing a consultant's interpretation of NICE guidance and have better connections in the medical profession to help them than the poor and marginalised. The best off have private health insurance.

Alternative systems of providing people with healthcare that avoid the NHS's collectivised allocation of resources are common in western Europe. France, Germany and Switzerland all operate systems of social insurance in which state subsidies are used to ensure universal coverage while giving patients more control over how they are treated.

Reform to give patients more power, while preserving the fundamental principle of the NHS that nobody should go without healthcare because they cannot afford it, could be achieved in a number of ways. In 2003, Reform proposed three steps to transform healthcare: changing the mission of the NHS to ensure that it was driven by individual patient need; (fully) liberating the supply side, transforming the NHS into a purchasing organisation, with money following the patient, freeing hospitals and other healthcare providers from NHS control and management; and reforming the demand side, or funding, either by giving entitlement portability, funded mainly by taxation, or through compulsory insurance.[156]

Risk-pooled health insurance administered through personal

---

156   'A Better Way', Reform, April 2003

health accounts, would put patients, not commissioning authorities, in control of the purse strings. This need not be expensive. For instance, under Ireland's pay-as-you-go, risk-pooled health insurance system, a basic plan which covers care in public and private hospitals and cover for outpatient medical expenses can be obtained for €1,033 (£825)[157] per year, which compares favourably with the NHS expenditure of more than £2,000 per person per year. As in most of continental Europe, people would be free to top their premiums up with their own resources.

A more far-reaching possibility, and the most financially sustainable model, is that of a Singapore-style health savings system, though a transition would take considerable time. As in Singapore, patients would choose to make higher contributions to build up larger funds to pay for private rooms and more comfortable conditions, but the core medical aspects of healthcare would be provided to all.

Providing a universal service in the form of personal health accounts (financed by current taxation or health savings), supplemented by top-ups that people can make out of their own resources, would transfer power over these vital parts of their own lives to people who haven't had it before. This would provide better results, patients would exercise more control, and the organisations from which they buy services would be forced to respond to their demands. This is a greater, and more important form of equality than that mandated by central fiat. A personalised NHS in which patients have greater control would be more readily re-focused on prevention, encouraging healthier lifestyles, which will be essential to reduce demand. It would also enable the necessary integration of health and social care.

The security which the NHS provides, eliminating worry about the means to pay medical bills, is prized in the UK. The Conservative

---

157 Quote obtained through the vhi.ie website; a small excess charge of €125 is applied to stays in private hospitals, and the first €250 of outpatient expenses is not covered – other health insurers offer competing products

Party will remain committed to the universal principles of the NHS that ensure this. But it is time to think ahead about how high-quality healthcare for all will be delivered in future through a reformed NHS. A system such as that which used to exist in the US (before 'Obamacare'), where some people find themselves without health insurance, would be wrong. But equitable systems of social insurance, as found elsewhere in Europe, are completely consistent with the ideals which the British public cherish and which form the basis of the NHS.

Against discrimination

Equality extends beyond equality of power over public services. Modern conservatism is resolutely opposed to discrimination. Though not always the dominant strain in Conservative practice, it has been present in our tradition for a long time. It is well known that Disraeli extended the franchise to working men and Emmeline Pankhurst stood as a Conservative parliamentary candidate, but our record is much more extensive.

From statutes limiting working hours in mines and factories, to some of the first attempts to improve the housing of the poor through the Artisans' and Labourers' Dwellings Improvement Act, Conservatives have led in social reform since the nineteenth century. Before the Liberal reforms undertaken prior to the First World War, Arthur Balfour's government passed the Unemployed Workmen Act in 1905. This addressed unemployment by setting up Distress Committees which were able to give temporary work or cash hand-outs to those in need. The 1920 and 1930s saw many significant reforms put in place by the administrations of Stanley Baldwin and Neville Chamberlain. One of the most important was the Widows, Orphans and Old Age Contributory Pensions Act from 1925 that saw pensions paid from the age of sixty-five, as well as the introduction of maintenance benefits for widows. The Holidays with Pay Act in 1938 was also the first piece of legislation to provide some workers with a period of paid holiday. Most significant of all, however, was the passing of the Equal Franchise Act of 1928, which finally gave all women over twenty-one the right to vote, ten years after the initial extension of the franchise.

It was a Conservative President of the Board of Education that got one of the most significant pieces of legislation of the twentieth century on the Statute Book. In 1944, R. A. Butler's Education Act provided free secondary education to all children and later saw the school leaving age raised to fifteen in 1948. Ten years later, as Chancellor of the Exchequer, Butler oversaw yet another important change when the government announced that it would press ahead with equal pay for women in the civil service. It is also little remembered that it was John Major's administration that passed the Disability Discrimination Act in 1995 – the first piece of UK legislation to ensure protection for disabled people from discrimination. Opposition to discrimination is thus squarely in our 'one nation' tradition, and the introduction of gay marriage is its natural continuation.

Equality is not the preserve of the left, whose attachment to collective provision tolerates persistent inequality. In seeking equality of power, it is progressive conservatism that can promote a true social justice.

Chapter 9

Opportunity

Opportunity has been a central theme of this government. In the words of the Prime Minister, addressing the Conservative Party conference in 2012:

> That's why the mission for this government is to build an aspiration nation ... to unleash and unlock the promise in all our people. And for ... Conservatives, this is not just an economic mission – it's also a moral one. It's not just about growth and GDP ... it's what's always made our hearts beat faster – aspiration; people rising from the bottom to the top. Line one, rule one of being a Conservative is that it's not where you've come from that counts, it's where you're going.

For Conservatives, there are two powerful reasons to improve opportunity: to help individuals to succeed, and to help the country to succeed. In Michael Gove's education reforms, the government may well have done more to promote opportunity than any administration has since council tenants were given the right to buy their homes. The reforms have begun to erode the educational dogma and grade inflation that has denied so many, often the poorest and most disadvantaged, the start in life that they deserve.

Good education is crucial to success and independence in today's technologically advanced economy. In Britain the best education is still too often restricted to the rich, either through private schools or through people having enough money to buy houses in areas near good schools. Decades of left-wing obsession with uniformity have failed millions through what George W. Bush so eloquently described as 'the soft bigotry of low expectations'.

Every attempt at reform has provoked opposition from vested interests. First direct grant schools, then grant-maintained schools, were abolished by Labour governments. Both free schools and academies, the latter effectively reintroduced by Labour and extended by Michael Gove, now face determined opposition from a left-wing educational establishment determined to deny parents choice over where their children are educated and to insulate schools from accountability. Too many children have been failed by a centralised system of provision.

Between 2000 and 2009 British pupils' performance on international standardised tests declined dramatically. Whereas in 2000 they averaged scores of 525 in reading and 530 in maths, by 2009, their results had fallen to 494 and 492 respectively.[158] The two principles that Conservatives should seek to promote are choice and rigour. Michael Gove's relentless championing of academies has paid off, with 1,700 primary schools and half of secondaries now benefiting from the independence that academies provide.[159] There are now 300 free schools and another hundred should open next year. Academies and free schools are promoting innovation and offering choice; the best state schools now achieve results as good as some of Britain's finest independent schools. As Michael Gove has said:

> Our fifteen-year-olds' results in maths, for example, were around three years behind their peers in Shanghai. But if you look just at England's very best schools – whether independent or state – that gap disappears. Our top schools are already performing just as well as Shanghai; just as well as the very best in the world.[160]

158 OECD, PISA Results, 2000 and 2009
159 Michael Gove, speech at the London Academy of Excellence, 3 February 2014
160 Ibid.

Labour would unpick these reforms, by imposing a new apparatus of regional school commissioners to deny schools the freedom to innovate and improve.[161] In office they allowed persistent grade inflation, which has deprived students of the opportunity to learn the skills and knowledge they need to compete in today's world. Its extent has been staggering. In 1989 the mark needed to achieve a grade C in the higher Oxford and Cambridge GCSE mathematics paper was 48 per cent. In 2000, it was 18 per cent.[162] Figures from *The Economist* for results at Westminster School show that the A level pass rate in 1988 was 40 per cent. By 1997 it had risen to 59 per cent, and by 2009 to 90 per cent.[163] Is it more likely that Westminster School improved its performance by more than a factor of two, or that A levels got significantly easier?

Michael Gove had begun to reverse this trend by creating the English Baccalaureate, to guide students to take the traditional subjects, including English, maths, foreign languages, science and history, that will serve them best when looking for work or applying to university. This summer, the proportion of A grades given out at A levels fell, and the pass rate has also fallen – for the first time in thirty years.[164] We should now go further. Young people deserve qualifications that employers and universities respect and understand. The best, and fairest, way to ensure the return of rigorous standards is to replace GCSCEs with a new examination.

Despite the government's reforms, the state still exerts considerable control over how schools are run, denying parents who cannot afford private schools' fees the choice and power possessed by the wealthy. Good schools are rationed by house price and admissions are still controlled. The British opposition to selective

---

161 Sean Coughlan, 'Labour wants a new tier of "Schools Standards tsars"', BBC News Online, 30 April 2004

162 'A Better Way', Reform, April 2003

163 'Explain away these examination results, then', *The Economist*, 16 August 2010

164 'A level grades edge down as university places rise', BBC News Online, 14 August 2014

education is almost unique. Virtually no other country operates a 'comprehensive' education system. Competitive entry examinations are used in countries like Germany and the Netherlands, and were championed by Soviet Russia. The aim should not be to recreate a replica of the grammar school and secondary modern system. Though it was more flexible than its left-wing detractors claim, its reintroduction would merely be to impose a different one-size-fits-all model of admissions. Rather, as the supply of new schools increases in each area, the admissions code could be reformed to allow diversity of provision and increased selection.

We should work towards a system of personal education accounts, allowing parents to top up the amount they pay, and should consider mechanisms of subsidised savings to enable more people to afford to invest in their children's education. For such a scheme to offer parents the widest possible choice, use of the personal education accounts should be allowed at schools run by mutuals and by providers who make a profit. Such providers would not worsen the quality of education, as the performance of independent schools demonstrates.

These reforms would put power in the hands of parents – just as the health reforms set out in Chapter 8 would put power in the hands of patients. They would give pupils from poorer backgrounds the kinds of opportunity that previously only the wealthy could envisage. They would break down the barriers between public and private provision, changing quite fundamentally the role of government. As the think tank Reform has said, 'Real reform should be based on widening choice, introducing competition and separating the role of the state as funder from the role of the state as provider. Because it means challenging existing ways of thinking and challenging vested interests, reform requires political commitment and leadership.'[165]

---

165 'Spending without Reform', Reform, June 2002

Higher and further education

The government has done much to promote higher education, both at academic and vocational levels. It will lift the cap on student numbers, allowing universities to supply courses in response to student demand not central government instruction, and British universities continue to punch above their weight in international rankings: there are eight British institutions in the Shanghai global top 100.[166] Immense progress has been made in vocational education, with the number of students starting apprenticeships in the UK each year more than doubling since the coalition took office. Five hundred thousand apprentices now start every year. The old claim that British vocational education is not good enough is no longer true. Hundreds of thousands of young people are acquiring practical skills every year, equipping them for today's competitive economy.

The government took the brave step of raising tuition fees at universities so that they come closer to reflecting the full cost of education, and allowing them to vary across institutions. This has not deterred students from applying to university.[167] It will provide strong incentives for universities to improve the quality of their teaching and, now that the government plans to lift the system by which places on particular courses are capped by officials, respond to student demand for courses. It is, furthermore, progressive. The system where people who did not go to university paid for the education of the people who benefited financially from it was untenable and socially unjust.

Enterprise and opportunity

A competitive economy thrives on entrepreneurship. One of the less discussed observations in Thomas Piketty's *Capital in the 21st*

---

166 http://www.shanghairanking.com/World-University-Rankings-2014/UK.html
167 Richard Adams, 'University tuition fee rise has not deterred poor students from applying', *The Guardian*, 13 August 2014

Century is that enterprise, not the heavy tax regime he favours, can overturn patterns of entrenched inequality. Entrepreneurs can upset established industries, or patterns within them. At the smaller scale, new neighbourhood businesses can bring prosperity to their owners and communities, at the expense of those who were formerly on top. Conservatives see enterprise as a vital mechanism of social justice. Entrepreneurial activity creates opportunity and undermines privilege. It is an engine of social mobility. It refreshes society and drives the economy. Entrepreneurial companies give people opportunities and responsibility that they could not acquire without years spent working for corporations, professions or in the public sector.

Though the legal process for setting up new businesses is straightforward, obstacles are still put in the way. Becoming self-employed makes it difficult to pass credit checks, let alone obtain a mortgage. Cultural opposition to entrepreneurship still exists on the left: witness their attempts to attack the government's economic record on the grounds that new jobs were created by people becoming self-employed. Access to finance remains a problem, particularly outside London in which the venture capital industry is concentrated. Though infinitely better equipped for enterprise than continental Europe, Britain is not yet a country with the entrepreneurial spirit of the United States or Israel. There is still too much stigma attached to failure. In the United States it is well understood that a successful entrepreneur is usually one who has failed before.

The government has pioneered the radical tax incentives of the Enterprise Incentive Scheme and the Seed Enterprise Investment Scheme that allow investors to reduce dramatically the taxes they have to pay if a start-up, always inherently risky, does not succeed. So far they have been presented as instruments to help the economy recover. But a surge in entrepreneurship should not be a one-off response to economic crisis: it needs to be a permanent feature of the British economy.

The job of any government is to ensure the stable macroeconomic conditions that enable businesses to thrive and create jobs, and the economy to grow. Since the government came to power, 400,000 businesses and over 2 million new jobs have been created.[168] The private sector has created five jobs for every one lost in the public sector.[169] In 2013, unemployment fell by 437,000 – the largest annual reduction in unemployment in twenty-five years. Youth unemployment fell by 206,000 – the largest drop since records began thirty years ago.[170] By contrast, when Labour left office, after presiding over the financial crisis, 428,000 more people were unemployed than when they came to power – an increase of over 20 per cent.[171]

At every general election the economy is the dominant issue. People will have to decide which party can be trusted to maintain the growth that has finally returned. Britain is now forecast to grow faster than any other major economy.[172] The Bank of England has upgraded its estimates for UK growth this year and next. It now predicts that the economy will grow by 3.5 per cent this year and 3 per cent next year.[173] The final chapter will examine the choice which the electorate faces between securing this economic success, and a better future for Britain, and putting it at risk.

---

168 ONS, Labour Market Statistics – Integrated FR – Public and private sector employment, August 2014
169 ONS, MFZ2, 11 June 2014
170 ONS, Labour Market Statistics, 13 August 2014
171 ONS, Labour Market Statistics, October 2011, Table A02
172 IMF, World Economic Outlook, 2014 Forecast
173 Bank of England, Inflation Report, 13 August 2014

Chapter 10

The Choice

The 2015 general election presents voters with a choice between two alternative governing philosophies: one is willing to accept the challenge of globalisation, prepared to equip Britain to take part in the global premier league that is being formed, and determined to undertake the reform necessary to achieve it; the other is hostile to the global economy, too focused on a conversation with its own ideological base, and committed to undoing the reforms the country needs.

A number of vital issues will be decided by the campaign. Will the British people have an in/out referendum on our membership of the European Union? Will education reforms be allowed to continue? Will Britain continue to engage with the world, or hide from it?

The main battle in May 2015 will, however, be fought on the economy. Will the next government continue to clear up after the financial crisis, put the public finances in order, and stimulate enterprise and the profit motive? Or will it return to fiscal profligacy, high taxes and a politically controlled economy?

Where Conservatives stand for fiscal responsibility and low taxes, Ed Miliband has made his intentions clear: his is the third stage of economic incompetence. The first stage is overspending, which the last Labour government did by hundreds of billions, if not a trillion pounds. The second stage is overtaxing: in office, Labour increased taxes by £1,400 per family, despite the successive years of economic growth.[174] Their plans for a future government have occasionally been revealed: Harriet Harman (Labour's deputy leader) let slip on the radio that 'people on middle incomes should contribute more through their taxes';[175] Andy Burnham (the shadow Health Secretary) said that Labour wanted a rise in national insurance to pay for the NHS; Ed Balls has proposed a £6 billion package of tax increases through a wealth tax, two years of levies on bankers' bonuses and (again) increasing the top rate of income tax to 50p;[176] Ed Miliband has opposed the government's cut in corporation tax.

The third stage of Labour's economic incompetence, and at least as dangerous, lies in the political management of the economy. Miliband believes that the financial crisis has created the perfect set of circumstances for politics to shift to the left, as people feel their incomes under pressure. He has concluded that it can justify not merely a New Labour-style agenda of redistribution in order to help the poor, but an Old Labour agenda undertaken for the purpose of attacking the rich.

Labour must justify this, because increasing public spending requires that the money be obtained from somewhere. With Public Sector Net Borrowing to be 6.6 per cent of GDP in 2013/14 and Public Sector Net Debt forecast to peak at 78.7 per cent of GDP in 2015/16,[177] there is little opportunity to borrow more, though Ed Balls plans to try by concealing higher borrowing for the purposes of capital spending.[178] Nor is it clear that higher taxes will raise more money. As the experience of the 50p top rate demonstrated, punitive taxes tend to produce a loss of revenue. As President Hollande has discovered in France, populist socialist pledges to squeeze the rich only harm the poor as the economy founders.

---

174   IFS, Tax and Benefit Reforms Under Labour, 7 April 2010
175   LBC phone-in programme, 14 July 2014
176   Financial Times, 10 March 2014
177   Office for Budget Responsibility, Economic and Fiscal Outlook, March 2014
178   'Ed Balls's surplus pledge leaves Labour for room to borrow to invest', New Statesman
        politics blog, 24 January 2014

A relatively responsible Labour economic policy would concentrate on returning the economy to growth so that the higher level of redistribution that they believe justified could be afforded. This was the model that Bill Clinton pursued in the United States. But Miliband has rejected this in favour of economic populism. His plan has two components. First, identify people in difficult economic circumstances: he initially called them the 'squeezed middle,' but now prefers the 'cost of living crisis'. Then, identify a target to blame, deem them guilty of predatory, rather than productive, capitalism, and promise to impose regulations on them to bring costs down.

Though Miliband has touched a public nerve, since people are worried that the prosperity generated by this wave of globalisation is beyond their reach, his distinction between producer and predator capitalism is drawn in the wrong place, while his solution of price controls by state command is inevitably counter-productive.

Addressing the Labour Party conference, he said: 'Let me tell you what the 21st-century choice is: are you on the side of the wealth creators or the asset strippers? The producers or the predators?'[179]

Miliband ostentatiously echoes Theodore Roosevelt, but when the 26th President attacked 'predatory' business, he knew precisely who his target was: monopolistic commerce that was acting against the consumer interest. Miliband has no idea who his 'asset strippers' are, and he will not say. Among the producers he identifies are 'British' companies like 'Bombardier and BAE systems' and Sheffield Forgemasters. Leave aside his difficulty ascertaining the nationality of the companies – Bombardier is Canadian, and its sophisticated engineering is done in Germany – all are firms whose principal business is winning government contracts. Bombardier's British operations chiefly make trains, BAE is an arms manufacturer, and Sheffield Forgemasters' expertise is concentrated in the largely state-owned power generation and defence sectors. Dynamic, entrepreneurial and technological companies are out.

179   Ed Miliband, speech to the Labour Party conference, 2011

Industry that depends on government contracts is in. To be qualified as a Miliband 'producer', a company needs to serve the state.

So far Miliband has named three targets for price controls: energy companies, train operators and landlords. Here is where the central planning comes unstuck. Among his 'producers' was Bombardier, the train manufacturers. Their ultimate customers[180] are train operators. But if train operators' prices are frozen, they will have less money available to order new trains, putting his favoured manufacturers out of work. The view that rent controls are self-defeating is as uncontroversial a statement as can be found in economics.[181] If they are imposed, a proportion of landlords will sell their properties instead, leaving less, not more, housing available to rent. And though there are indeed problems in the energy market, they would not be solved by the imposition of unworkable price controls in place of proper regulation.

Every time political considerations cause Miliband to pick a business sector, the effects of his intervention will be counterproductive. Worse, they create fear among businesses in all other areas of the economy that they might become politically unpopular and targeted next. There is no criterion, other than political expediency, that guides Miliband's selection of industries. In these circumstances, the entire management of the economy is susceptible to unpredictable politicisation. At least communist command economies were directed towards a conception of the national interest. Miliband's command economy would be directed by political expediency.

Miliband does not understand the 'Square Deal' which Theodore Roosevelt offered. Roosevelt condemned 'government primarily for the benefit of one class instead of a government for the benefit of the

---

180 Technically the trains are sold to leasing firms known as ROSCOs or to financing vehicles under government direction, because trains last longer than franchises so they have to be leased to operators

181 The seminal work on rent control is Milton Friedman and George Steigler, 'Roofs or Ceilings', Foundation for Economic Education, 1946

people as a whole.'[182] Miliband's regulatory socialism brings a government run by the political class, for the political class, considerably closer.

That Labour has become anti-business again owes a great deal to how its leader was elected – by union votes – and its sources of funding. The party received more than £8 million from the trade unions in 2013.[183] Trade unions are determined to exert influence in return. In the words of Len McLuskey, General Secretary of UNITE, 'I'm as keen as anyone, as you've probably noticed, on debating Labour policy. But I want to have those debates with Ed Miliband in No. 10, not in opposition.'[184] The teaching unions have forced Labour to undo Michael Gove's reforms. Labour have now said they will institute regional schools commissioners to oversee academies, leaving them less free than when Gordon Brown was Prime Minister. Labour's education spokesman, Tristram Hunt, has been forced to defend restrictions on teachers that would require him to give up teaching classes in his own constituency.[185]

Miliband's support for 'producers' seems apt for a leader whose instinct is to side with the producer interest in public services rather than its users. The contrast with Tony Blair, who even spoke of 'the scars on [his] back' from trying to reform the public sector, is striking. Miliband is hostile to private sector provision in healthcare. He has opposed reforms to policing. It is impossible to conceive that he would either have the strength or the inclination to withstand the claims of the public sector unions if he were in government.

Nor has he shown any understanding of the tough decisions that will be needed to manage the public finances. Under his leadership Labour has opposed welfare reforms, including the cap on benefits. Since June 2013, the frontbench of the Labour Party have made policy

182 Speech to farmers at the New York State Agricultural Association, Syracuse, New York, 7 September 1903
183 Labour Party Statement of Accounts 2013. Accessed on the Electoral Commission website
184 Unite conference, 30 June 2014
185 Toby Young, 'Hunt's 12 Most Embarrassing Gaffes', *Daily Telegraph*, 3 April 2014

commitments that would cost £27.9 billion in the first year of a Labour government. This is the equivalent of £1,059 additional borrowing for every household.[186]

Ed Miliband and his shadow Chancellor, Ed Balls, were Gordon Brown's key advisers. They have neither recanted nor changed. They still believe, as Brown believed, in spending, borrowing and taxing more. These are the policies that caused Britain to go into the financial crisis with a deficit, and leave with the largest deficit in peacetime history. They cannot be trusted to run the economy again.

UKIP

Despite the fact that Labour has ruled out a referendum on the EU, they may be greatly assisted at the next election by UKIP which, if it takes too many votes from Conservative candidates in marginal seats, could deprive the Conservatives of a majority, or even deny us from forming a government. It is true that UKIP is also taking votes from Labour, but it is doing more damage to the Conservatives; indeed, that seems to be its aim.

UKIP wants to leave the EU. They want a referendum on Britain's membership. And yet they are opposing the only party that could deliver that referendum. With a Conservative government, there would be a referendum in no more than three years' time. UKIP's holy grail is in sight. They seem determined to make the event less likely.

What is the logic that lies behind this apparently suicidal strategy? UKIP's leader, Nigel Farage, says that it is a matter of trust. He repeatedly claims that David Cameron reneged on his 'cast-iron guarantee' to hold a referendum on the Lisbon Treaty, and that a Conservative government could not therefore be trusted to deliver the promised in/out referendum. But it was Labour who were in power at the time and who, in breach of their promise, ratified the Treaty. David Cameron's

---

186 'Same Old Labour's Budget for Borrowing', Conservative Party, October 2013

argument is that he did not pledge to hold a referendum once the Treaty was ratified, and could never have held such a referendum after the fact.

By contrast, the promise to hold an in/out referendum will be in the Conservative Party's manifesto. Almost every Conservative MP has already voted in the House of Commons to try and write the pledge into law, although the Bill was scuppered by Labour and the Liberal Democrats. The next Conservative government will be bound by its MPs to hold the referendum; there is no doubt, should we be elected, that one will be held. The party would brook no other outcome.

There is, of course, an important difference between UKIP and the Conservative Party. UKIP want to leave the EU come what may. That is not Conservative policy, which is to renegotiate Britain's terms of membership and put a better deal to the public in a referendum. But the referendum is UKIP's only chance to secure their objective, and in the end the people will decide.

UKIP is a single-issue party and a vehicle for protest. They have little interest in other matters. On the most important issue facing Britain, managing the economy competently and getting the public finances in order, they have nothing coherent to say. Their spending plans are £120 billion short, almost the cost of the bank bail-out.[187] In trying to win support from both traditional Labour supporters as well as Conservatives, their contradictions will only increase. They want to increase and reduce spending on the NHS.[188] They complain about the 'soaring benefits bill' but condemn welfare reform as 'heartless and punitive'.[189] They want to 'enhance' pensions but cannot guarantee they will rise.[190] They have nothing to offer anyone interested in making responsible decisions about the future of our country – except that we should leave the EU. From this single change, all else will flow.

---

187 'A £120bn black hole behind the dream of a better Britain', *The Times*, 29 April 2013
188 *Daily Telegraph*, 28 January 2014; campaign literature for John Bickley, UKIP candidate in Wythenshawe & Sale East by-election, February 2014
189 *Sunderland Echo*, 6 June 2013; *Daily Telegraph*, 28 January 2014
190 Tim Aker's 2013 conference speech, YouTube, 21 September 2013; Suzanne Evans, Twitter, 28 April 2014

Only, they will do whatever they now can to prevent the referendum needed to achieve it.

UKIP has tapped into genuine concern about immigration among voters. The failure of the major political parties to address these concerns, and a political correctness that has denied sensible debate about the failures of multiculturalism, has undoubtedly allowed UKIP to step into the void. The party has recruited the support of large numbers of voters who are not racist, but it is a dreadful vehicle for their reasonable concerns. UKIP is an angry party. It oozes a loathing of contemporary Britain. It is backward-looking and isolationist. One UKIP councillor blamed storms and floods on the introduction of gay marriage. One of its MEPs calls women 'sluts'. Another activist quit the party, accusing it of descending 'into a form of racist populism'. [191]

Eventually, UKIP will kill the cause it sets out to promote. In the meantime, it is enjoying the success of an insurgency. It is capitalising on the insecurity caused by the economic downturn and the mood of anti-politics in the country. The Conservative Party must hold its nerve. Any kind of bargain with UKIP, which some have suggested, would be Faustian, the opportunity of wider appeal sold for illusory political gain. Like two bitter old bores drinking together in a pub, no one else would want to talk to us.

It is true that the Conservative Party needs to reach out beyond its core to obtain a winning share of the national vote, but the overture should be to electors in the north, to women, to ethnic minorities, to a generation who are working ever harder for seemingly less reward.

This is the grand coalition that Conservatives must forge. At its most powerful our party has appealed beyond the shires to the cities, to those who want to get on as much as to those who have already succeeded, to the young as well as the elderly. It has captured an optimism about our country, rewarded aspiration and challenged privilege. We must not be spooked by a minority party or emulate a politics that will drive moderate voters away.

Liberal Democrats

Another party once enjoyed political insurgency. The SDP was formed in 1981 to 'break the mould' of British politics. At its peak it enjoyed 50 per cent support in the opinion polls and, in alliance with the Liberals, it won nine by-elections. Twenty-eight Labour MPs and one Conservative MP joined the new party. The SDP–Liberal Alliance won more than 25 per cent of the national vote in the 1983 general election, not far behind Labour's 28 per cent, but this fell to 23 per cent in the 1987 election, and the number of SDP MPs was reduced from eight to five. In 1988 the parties merged, becoming known as the Liberal Democrats the following year.

Neither David Owen nor his fellow members of the 'Gang of Four' who formed the SDP, all of whom had been senior Labour ministers, were ever to return to government. Yet their successors in the Liberal Democrats, probably to their great surprise, found themselves in government when the coalition was formed in 2010. We should credit their leaders for taking that responsible decision when the country needed a strong and stable government to tackle the economic crisis. There has been little to credit them with since.

Though the Liberal Democrats have co-operated with us on deficit reduction, they have undermined some of the government's most crucial reforms. They have put sand in the gears of Michael Gove's educational reforms, blocking the replacement of GCSEs with a new qualification, and diverting funds from teaching and learning by insisting on an unnecessary and bureaucratic requirement for all schools to provide free meals, even for children of affluent parents. They have obstructed employment law reforms. They have prevented us curtailing the rights culture by blocking attempts to scrap the Human Rights Act. They reneged on the agreement to introduce boundary reform, despite it being in the coalition agreement, and prevented the government from embarking on a renegotiation of our relationship with the EU. They killed the EU Referendum Bill and half killed police and crime commissioners, another policy in the coalition agreement. Naturally, they opposed a reduction in the top rate of income tax to 40p.

Nick Clegg boasted of the policies he had blocked in government when he addressed his party conference in 2013. He had prevented reductions in inheritance tax and the immediate renewal of Trident. He had stymied cuts to green subsidies and freedom for free schools. His speech was a celebration of the obstructive exercise of power. They require every decision in government to be traded. The Liberal Democrats once existed to oppose every other party, and had little need of policies of their own. Now they exist to frustrate one party as its coalition partner. They do not mind which.

The Liberal Democrats aspire to the position they sought when they tried to change Britain's voting system: permanent members of the political class, constantly in power whatever the result at a general election. At present, this party that has abandoned any trace of principle has been rewarded with an opinion poll rating well below 10 per cent. It is richly deserved.

Why vote Conservative?

The immediate argument for a Conservative government is that it will continue to fix the public finances, reduce taxes, and stimulate entrepreneurship and growth. Unlike every Labour administration, Conservative governments do not run out of money. The longer-term argument is that only a Conservative government can equip Britain to meet the challenges of globalisation; ensure that education is reformed so that everyone will be able to benefit from the opportunities it offers; institute the political reform required to allow people to fulfil their duty to hold the government to account; place social security on a sound long-term footing; reform healthcare to put patients in charge; and maintain an active international involvement to secure the country and promote prosperity abroad.

Every election presents a choice, and there are many reasons to fear the alternatives. Labour would undo all that has been achieved to restore our country's economic fortunes, returning to the failed policies of more spending, borrowing and taxes. Every vote for UKIP, whose angry nationalism would divide our country, would only help Labour and deny the opportunity of the EU referendum which the Conservative Party has pledged. The Liberal Democrats, devoid of principle, seek only to hold the balance of power.

These are, indeed, all good reasons for voting Conservative. But there is a more powerful case to be made. Politics must have a purpose, power must be exercised for a reason, and politicians must give a lead. It will not be enough for Conservatives to warn of the consequences of a change of government, true though the risk is. We must set out the challenges facing our country, explain why change is needed, and supply a bold programme to achieve it.

Britain in the twenty-first century has immense potential. With our national power we can do great good in the world. With a strong economy we can spread wealth and prosperity. With reform we can give people ownership and opportunities that their parents could scarcely have dreamed of. With resolve we can ensure security. With determination we can change the course of Europe. With foresight we can protect our environment for future generations.

This book has proposed a radical Conservative agenda to reform our political institutions, including the EU, and address concerns about immigration; to enhance national security; to bring government closer to the people, including through devolution in England; to reform welfare so that it is based on contributions; to transform schools and the NHS through personal education and health accounts; and to lower taxes.

These policies are founded on Conservative values – nation, security, liberty, community, equality and opportunity – that have ensured the party's success for the better part of the last hundred years. If we apply these values today, we will win the public's trust to build another Conservative century.

Appendix 1

Ten Conservative Achievements

1. Cutting the deficit and restoring the economy

The deficit will have halved by 2015 and will be eliminated by 2017, when debt will be falling. Britain now has the fastest growth of any major industrialised country.

2. Cutting taxes

Over twenty-five million people have received a typical tax cut of £700 and over three million people have been taken out of tax altogether. Fuel duty has been frozen and is now more than 13p per litre lower than it would have been, saving the average family over £7 every time they fill up their tank. Corporation tax has been cut to a highly competitive 20 per cent and an employers' national insurance allowance of £2,000 is helping businesses.

3. Creating more jobs

There are two million more private sector jobs and 400,000 more businesses. Unemployment is falling faster than at any time in the last quarter of a century.

4. Capping welfare

No out-of-work household can now claim more than the average working family earns, ensuring that the economy delivers for people who want to work hard and play by the rules.

5. Reforming schools and improving skills

Over 4,000 schools are now benefiting from the freedoms of academy status and standards are being raised. More than 1.8 million new apprenticeships have been created.

6. Helping people to own their own homes

Nearly half a million homes have been built, while 48,000 families have bought their homes under 'help to buy'.

7. Protecting the NHS

There are 7,000 more doctors, 4,000 more nurses and 19,000 fewer administrators in the NHS. A £1.1 billion Cancer Drugs Fund has helped more than 55,000 people. 850,000 more operations are being performed annually and fewer people are waiting more than eighteen weeks for an operation.

8. Making the streets safe

Crime is down by more than 10 per cent, to its lowest level since records began, showing that services can improve despite budget reductions. Elected police and crime commissioners have replaced invisible and toothless police authorities, making policing more accountable to local communities.

9. Cutting the EU budget

The EU budget has been cut and the Prime Minister vetoed a new EU Fiscal Treaty, standing up for British interests and saving taxpayers money.

10. Controlling immigration

Net migration has been reduced by a quarter from its peak under Labour. Immigration from outside the EU has been reduced by 50,000 to levels not seen since the late 1990s. More than 700 bogus colleges have been closed and the number of student visas has been reduced by more than a quarter. There are now language tests for visas for non-EU immigrants. EU immigrants' access to benefits is being limited.

Appendix 2

Conservative Values and Policy Proposals

1. Nation

Disraeli said that 'the Tory party, unless it is a national party, is nothing'. But we are not nationalists. We are proud of our country and know what makes Britain great, but are practical about our national interest.

We are the Conservative and Unionist Party. If Scotland votes to leave the Union, it will be a shock to the UK, but we will recover and prosper, while an independent Scotland, living beyond its means and in the grip of a socialist utopian fantasy, will face rising taxes, spending cuts and long-term decline. Divorce should be amicable, but cannot be on Scotland's terms. They cannot share the pound, and MPs for Scottish constituencies cannot be permitted to allow the formation of a UK government in the 2015 general election.

If Scotland remains in the Union, there should be further devolution throughout the UK, including in England, where there must be at least English votes for English laws. A more radical alternative would be a fully federal UK with an English Parliament.

To build 'one nation', the economic gap between London and the English regions should be closed with radical measures, including designating Britain's major cities outside London as large-scale enterprise zones.

A reform agenda for the EU should aim to make Europe more competitive, protect the City of London, and allow countries to reject 'ever closer union'. It should enable Britain to manage migration by allowing us to deny entry to criminals and require people who move countries to remain attached to their own welfare system until they have contributed to ours, and capping excessive migration flows. If there is sufficient reform to the EU it will remain in our national interest to stay in. If we cannot secure satisfactory changes, especially in relation to immigration, we should be prepared to leave.

2. Security

Conservatives are not libertarians. Ensuring the security of the citizen is the first duty and primary function of government. People need security from criminals but also from illness and misfortune. Our environmental security will also become increasingly important.

Britain needs a muscular foreign policy, with strong armed forces and a willingness to intervene to prevent serious crimes against humanity, support democracy and ensure international security.

Personal security and the fight against crime should be promoted through radical penal reform, 'honest' sentences, new overnight detention centres combined with curfewing, and the creation of an officer cadre in the police.

The responsibility to protect the environment should be a thoroughly Conservative principle, but environmentalism made itself at home chiefly on the left. 'Red-Green' policies are ineffective and impose excessive regulation and cost on businesses and consumers. Our environmental security should be promoted through 'Blue-Green' policies which embrace technology, incentives, competition and markets.

Conservatives should promote security through ownership. Incentives to invest in shared ownership properties could help people onto the property ladder, while social tenants' rents could be converted to mortgage payments to allow them to build a share of their properties through a new 'right to own'. Neighbourhood planning should be strengthened. Major new developments such as garden cities could have an important role in providing new homes, but unsustainable new towns should not be imposed without local consent. A new system of community auctions to release land should be explored, and self-build increased.

The pay-as-you-go system of pensions should be replaced so that responsibility is rewarded and saving is encouraged through personal savings accounts to provide better security in retirement.

3. Liberty

The rights culture has undermined our traditional conception of liberty. We should withdraw from the European Court of Human Rights and replace the Human Rights Act with a British Bill of Rights and Responsibilities.

Conservatives should stand as firmly against unethical business and monopoly as we do for the virtue of profit. Taxes, not profits, are the necessary evil, and they always reduce freedom. Spending must be controlled to lower taxes. The priority for a Conservative Party that seeks to govern for one nation must be to cut taxes for those on lower and middle incomes. Taxes should be lower, simpler and flatter.

Government should be 'quiet' – interfering no more than is necessary – and made more efficient. Whitehall should be radically reformed, including a reduction in the number of ministers and government departments.

4. Community

Modern Conservatism emphasises the importance of community as much as individual liberty. That is why Conservatives should be serious about devolving power. Individuals should have more power through greater choice in public services and personal budgets. Communities should have more power through schemes like the 'Neighbourhood Takes Charge' programme.

English government remains excessively centralised. We should push again, more effectively and with conviction, for localism. Directly elected mayors for cities should have more powers and more responsibility for raising local revenue. Police and crime commissioners should become police and justice commissioners, with powers over probation and local justice services, as well as 'blue light' emergency services, which could become increasingly integrated at the local level. Police forces should not be amalgamated; if anything, stronger national policing should allow for smaller forces which are more closely connected to local communities.

Conservatives identify with institutions and assets such as our heritage and the countryside. We must beware of a kind of cold Conservatism, a cousin to unbridled liberalism, that limits an appreciation of these things to their economic value.

Conservatives do not believe that compassion can be measured by how much public money is spent. We should be sceptical of pledges to meet arbitrarily set targets to spend at particular levels, being more interested in the effectiveness of spending and its outcomes. But our international aid programme has saved millions of lives and is profoundly moral. Compassionate conservatism should be the hallmark of our party today.

5. Equality

Conservatives reject the left's conception of equality enforced through collective provision. We seek to give the poor an equality of power over essential services that is currently enjoyed only by the wealthy.

Public services should be accountable to their users, yet patients have no power in the NHS, which in effect rations care. Rising health demands will not be met in the future through the existing system, nor is higher taxation to fund more spending or the introduction of charges the answer.

The NHS should be transformed to allow more health services to be supplied to patients by independent providers, and by giving all patients health insurance (as found across continental Europe) through personal health accounts. This would give patients more control and enable more personalised healthcare, while maintaining the ideal of a universal service.

6. Opportunity

Conservative school reforms, to improve standards and give schools more freedom, may have done more to promote opportunity than any policy since the 'right to buy' council houses. We must continue with reforms that are essential to fulfil potential and ensure the country's success.

To maintain the drive for higher standards, GCSEs should be replaced with a rigorous new exam. As the supply of new schools increases in each area, the admissions code could be reformed to allow diversity of provision and increase selection. We should work towards a system of personal education accounts, allowing parents to top up the amount they pay. The accounts would be allowed at schools run by mutuals and for profit. These reforms would put power in the hands of parents, extend choice and break down the barriers between public and private provision.

Acknowledgements

This book inevitably reflects views that I have formed in different roles over the past decades. At Business for Sterling, I led the formation of the 'no' campaign against joining the euro, which adopted the slogan 'Europe, yes; euro, no'. We were told then that this was an impossible choice; that Britain had to decide whether we wanted to be in the eurozone or out of the EU altogether. In fact, it proved perfectly possible to be in the single market while retaining our currency. Today, we are being told that Britain must choose between ever closer union or exit. I believe we must show that this, too, is false.

In 2001 I started a new think tank, Reform, with Andrew Haldenby. Initially working on our own laptops in an empty office, we seemed to be lonely voices at a time when the political zeitgeist was to 'choose fairness', to use the IPPR's phrase, which actually meant increasing public spending. Tax revenues have not matched state spending in a single year since, producing debt that is the greatest unfairness of all. But our mission was far more than to warn of the dangers of 'spending without reform': it was to attack privilege and widen opportunity.

We set out ideas to extend school choice, bringing over educationalists from the US and Sweden to talk about how they had given new chances to children from poorer backgrounds. We worked with doctors to urge new ways to deliver and fund healthcare, including through social insurance. We proposed new ways to improve the accountability and efficiency of policing. Some of these ideas found their way into modern Conservative thinking and the current government's reform agenda; others did not. But I remain driven by the same convictions, and have referred to Reform's work in this book.

After I was elected to the House of Commons in 2005, I drew up the Conservative Party's proposals for police and justice reform, and was proud to help put them in place in government. The experience informed me about the power of vested interests, about the challenge of overcoming inertia, and that the careful use of political organisation matters as much as having good ideas. But it also taught me that it is possible to translate a bold political vision into a radical set of policy proposals and successfully implement them.

Early in my first job, in 1986, I helped our candidate in the West Derbyshire by-election, Patrick McLoughlin, who won what had been a safe Conservative seat by just 100 votes. That night, across the Pennines, we lost another constituency that we had previously held with a big majority. The next day the Prime Minister, Mrs Thatcher, paid an unusual visit to Conservative Central Office to steady the ship. She told us that the party wouldn't just win the next election, but also the one after that (she was, of course, right). But, she continued, since we could not expect to go on winning indefinitely, we needed to replace the Labour Party with one that believed in fundamentally the same things as we did, a party such as the Democrats in the United States. Her mission, she told us, was now to 'destroy socialism'.

I am not sure, until that moment, that I had fully understood the significance of Mrs Thatcher. In one short, off-the-cuff speech, displaying her qualities of courage, leadership and vision, she electrified me. It is a mistake to believe that a Conservative generation only learned from her the value of liberal economics (important though that was). She taught us about purpose in politics.

I would like to thank the members of my team who have helped me over the years and with this book. I would also like to thank members of the Arundel & South Downs Conservative Association for selecting me for, and the electorate for allowing me the privilege of representing, the best constituency in England. It is here, every week, that I am reminded why I am a Conservative.

About the Author

Nick Herbert has been the Conservative MP for Arundel & South Downs since May 2005. He went to school at Haileybury, from where he won an Open Exhibition to read Law and Land Economy at Magdalene College, Cambridge.

He worked in the Conservative Research Department and for the British Field Sports Society, playing a leading role in setting up the Countryside Movement, which became the Countryside Alliance.

He stood in the 1997 general election as the Conservative parliamentary candidate in Berwick Upon Tweed, and then became chief executive of Business for Sterling, where he launched the successful 'no' campaign against the euro, before co-founding the independent think tank Reform.

In opposition he served as shadow Minister for Police Reform, shadow Secretary of State for Justice and shadow Secretary of State for Environment, Food and Rural Affairs. He was Minister of State for Policing and Criminal Justice, working in both the Home Office and Ministry of Justice, for the first two and half years of the coalition government, where he led radical reforms to policing.

He played a leading role in the successful campaign for equal marriage, setting up Freedom to Marry. He also takes a strong interest in the problem of tuberculosis, and is co-chairman of the All Party Parliamentary Group on Global TB. This year he co-founded GovernUp, a cross-party initiative to promote the far-reaching reforms needed in Whitehall and beyond to enable more effective and efficient government.

He lives in Arundel with his partner, Jason Eades.